D1452634

THE GUNNER AND THE GRUNT

THE GUNNER AND THE GRUNT

Two Boston Boys in Vietnam with
the First Cavalry Division Airmobile

MICHAEL L. KELLEY AND PETER BURBANK

CASEMATE

Philadelphia & Oxford

Published in the United States of America and Great Britain in 2023 by
CASEMATE PUBLISHERS
1950 Lawrence Road, Havertown, PA 19083, USA
and
The Old Music Hall, 106–108 Cowley Road, Oxford OX4 1JE, UK

Previous edition published in 2020 by King Printing Company.

Hardback Edition: ISBN 978-1-63624-343-6
Digital Edition: ISBN 978-1-63624-344-3

A CIP record for this book is available from the British Library

Printed and bound in the United Kingdom by CPI Group (UK) Ltd, Croydon, CR0 4YY

Typeset in India by Lapiz Digital Services, Chennai.

For a complete list of Casemate titles, please contact:

CASEMATE PUBLISHERS (US)
Telephone (610) 853-9131
Fax (610) 853-9146
Email: casemate@casematepublishers.com
www.casematepublishers.com

CASEMATE PUBLISHERS (UK)
Telephone (0)1226 734350
Email: casemate-uk@casematepublishers.co.uk
www.casematepublishers.co.uk

Dedication

This book is dedicated to my wife, soul mate, and best friend, Ruth Frances (Nardone) Kelley, who stood by me for 48 faithful years until her death in 2018; to my loving son, Richard James Kelley, who died in 2002; and to all of my comrades who served with the 1st Squadron, 9th Cavalry (Recon), 1st Cavalry Division (Airmobile).

Soldier

I was that which others did not want to be.
I went where others feared to go, and did what others
failed to do.
I asked nothing from those who gave nothing, and reluctantly
accepted the thought of eternal loneliness… should I fail.
I have seen the face of terror; felt the stinging cold of fear;
and enjoyed the sweet taste of a moment's love.
I have cried, pained, and hoped… but most of all,
I have lived times others would say were best forgotten.
At least someday,
I will be able to say that I was proud of
what I was… a soldier.

Written by George L. Skypeck, Combat Veteran,
Captain, U.S. Army
© Captain George L. Skypeck

Contents

You can never have too much reconnaissance.
General George S. Patton, Third Army, World War II

Acknowledgements

Special thanks to those who supported my long struggle to write this book despite my 50-year battle with PTSD and the grief I still deal with over the loss of my wife and 27-year-old son, Richard James Kelley. To Dr. Douglas Gammon, PhD, and Dr. Heidi Lilienthal, PhD, both retired from the Veterans Administration Hospital at Bedford, Massachusetts. Thanks for your compassion and support during my dark days.

I would also like to thank Chloe Longstreet, my freelance editor, who edited and polished this manuscript for publication; and Robin Wrighton, who designed the original book cover.

Finally, I want to thank all of the brave veterans of the 9th Cavalry who provided me with information, photos, and memories of their service in the Vietnam War. To those readers who like this book, I want to thank you for learning about a soldier's life in the Vietnam War. I grew up on books about World War II and Korean War Veterans, and I hope there is a younger generation out there who will read about the veterans of the Vietnam, Afghanistan, and Iraq Wars.

If you're going through hell, keep going.
—Winston Churchill, World War II

Prologue

The Lost Gunship

December 12, 1965.

"Kelley, from now on, don't carry your wallet when you go out on recon missions." The weapons platoon sergeant smiled and put his hand on my shoulder.

"Why?"

"We lost a gunship last month in the Ia Drang Valley. If you get shot down like they did, we don't want the enemy to get their hands on your personal stuff, understand?"

"I understand."

His words filled me with fear. Later that evening, the door gunners and crew chiefs returned to the tent and began to unwind from a long day of flying combat assault missions in support of the infantry brigade battalions. I was a new man, a "Cherry, still pissing stateside water." They sat on their cots, smoking cigarettes and playing cards under the single 60-watt bulb hanging from the center tent pole.

I watched and listened, trying my best to learn about who these guys were and where I fit in. So far, it seemed like I didn't. To make things worse, I was much younger than they were. Most had been in the Army a couple of years or longer. They ignored me as they joked and talked about some of the missions they had flown in past battles, especially the recent campaign in the Ia Drang Valley.

These men were hardened combat veterans who had seen much death and destruction. I was afraid to talk to them, but my curiosity about the

"Lost Gunship" overcame my fear. I wanted to know more about this ghost story that was haunting me. Surely, I could ask someone.

Specialist Four Bill Clark was sitting on his cot with a cigarette hanging off his lips, sharpening his bayonet with a special stone. Something about his manner made him seem more approachable. Maybe it was because he was alone.

"Could you tell me about the gunship that got lost in Ia Drang last month?"

"Sure kid, I'll tell you about the Lost Gunship." He pulled a drag from his cigarette and eyed me with amusement.

"One of our air crews were out screening the flanks of the 3rd Brigade somewhere in the vast Ia Drang Valley when they came across some enemy and took them under fire. The North Vietnamese troops shot their Huey gunship down with automatic weapons fire. All four crewmen were killed."

He looked away and continued to make his bayonet razor sharp. Clark was a man of few words and his story was brief and lacking in detail. I went back to my cot feeling immensely dissatisfied and wondering what the fate of those four crewmen had been.

I did not learn the full story until many years later, while attending one of my unit's reunions. I was talking with some of my old pilots, Dick Marshall and Johnny Gower. Both Marshall and Gower were retired Army officers with long careers flying helicopters and if anyone knew the story of the Lost Gunship, it would be these two pilots; they were there when it went down.

On November 16, 1965, (about three weeks before I arrived in-country at An Khe Base Camp), Troop C was flying out of the Duc Co Special Forces Camp north of the Ia Drang, attached to the 3rd Brigade, 1st Cavalry Division (Airmobile), which was engaged in deadly ground combat with the North Vietnamese Army's (NVA) B-3 Front Division near the Chu Pong mountain in the valley. This was the very first major battle of the Vietnam War.

Marshal was flying one of two Huey gunships on a screening and recon support mission to make sure the enemy did not outflank the brigade's infantry. With him were two "Little Birds," OH-13S Sioux Aero Scout recon helicopters, flying low level just above the treetops, looking for signs of the enemy. Gower was a pilot on one of the Little Birds. The other gunship with Marshall was his chase ship, piloted by Warrant Officers Billy J. Talley and Benedicto P. Bayron. Door gunners Sergeant James L. Riley and Specialist Five Billy M. Knight were also on board.

Talley called Marshall on the radio and told him they were low on fuel and were going to return to Duc Co to refuel. Somewhere along their flightpath back to Duc Co, while at treetop level, they encountered NVA forces under the jungle canopy. They sent a radio message to the command post (CP) at Duc Co that they were going to engage the enemy. That was the last radio contact the troop had with the gunship. Talley's door gunners fired their M-60 door guns briefly before the NVA managed to shoot the gunship down in the fast-running firefight.

"I always believed the pilots were hit by automatic weapons fire which made them lose control of their ship, and crash." I wondered how many times Marshall had thought of those moments in the years since returning home.

Eventually, Marshall's gunship and the two Scout birds returned to Duc Co for fuel and ammo, before quickly flying back to the battlefield to conduct a search for their lost crewmen. They tried to make radio contact with Warrant Officer Talley, but there was no response from the gunship. Scout pilot Captain Johnny Gower and his Scout observer gunner were flying low and slow over the jungle in a grid fashion over the general area where it was estimated the gunship went down. Eventually, Gower and his Scout observer spotted the wreckage of the gunship in a small jungle clearing, laying on its side. Gower pulled up his radio.

"I found it. The Huey looks like it made a hard landing and rolled over. I'm going to try to land and make a ground search for the crewmen."

The trees were high and thickly forested, but Gower was a very experienced and skillful aviator. He managed to find an open spot and lowered his Little Bird down to the jungle floor. He kept his engine on and his rotors turning in case he needed to make a quick escape in the event of an enemy attack. He was deep inside NVA territory, a place the troops called "Indian Country."

"Make a search to the west side of the wreckage for any signs of the crewmen," Gower told his Scout observer as he looked at the Huey and noticed that the machine guns were still mounted on the aircraft. He then began to search towards the east of the ship. At the edge of a clearing, he saw one of the pilots sitting up against a tree. The pilot had been shot in the head by the NVA and was bleeding all over, having sustained various injuries in the crash. The Scout observer spotted the other pilot in the same condition. They did not find the two door gunners.

Above them, circling overhead, was Marshall's gunship and the other OH-13S Scout "Little Bird" keeping a sharp eye out for enemy movement. Captain James Kidd, Marshall's co-pilot, spotted NVA troops on a nearby hill. He called down to Gower on the radio to warn them, but Gower and his Scout observer did not hear the call because they were outside their aircraft looking around.

"All of a sudden, I began to get a 'spooky' feeling that I was being watched." Gower shivered as he remembered the feeling that was still so vivid to him, even years later.

Gower yelled at his observer to get back into the helicopter and just as he started to do the same, the NVA began to fire in his direction from the jungle. Gower jumped into his Little Bird and quickly powered up the 260 horsepower Lycoming engine for takeoff. Just then he heard Captain Kidd on the radio.

"Thirsty White, this is Thirsty Red. Get out of there now! Enemy on your left flank!"

"Roger that, Red!"

Of course, Gower already knew the enemy was near as he had received their calling card, a burst of automatic weapons fire. He rolled the throttle control and brought his Little Bird up to full maximum power and then pulled up on the collective control for a straight vertical takeoff. This was the most stressful kind of takeoff for any helicopter, especially in a tropical environment where even a normal takeoff can be dangerous. As the NVA closed in for the kill, the little Sioux Warrior climbed up through the jungle canopy. As Gower cleared the treetops, he swung his bird around and lowered the nose, firing a long burst from his twin

M-60C 7.62mm outboard machine guns at the enemy. That suppressive fire was just enough for him to make his getaway.

The Little Bird sprang forward and took off like an African Gazelle. Marshall had his door gunners open up on the enemy below to keep them at bay. Gower called back to the CP at Duc Co and gave them the estimated position of the downed Huey, while Troop Commander Major Billy Williams called in an Air Force airstrike to drop napalm onto the lost Huey gunship in order to destroy it. A few weeks later, an aero rifle platoon from Troop B located the remains of the dead gunship crewmen and brought them back to the base camp.

Rumors spread all over the 1st Cavalry Division that the gunship crewmen had been mutilated and tortured by the enemy. Those kinds of stories only made crewmen like me very nervous and scared. In reality, the bodies had probably been attacked by the many wild jungle animals, insects, and other "creepy" things on the jungle floor, causing them to appear as though they had been mutilated.

The facts of this story were related to me by these two very brave pilots. I will never forget them or the memories of the fear I carried with me during my tour of duty in Vietnam as an Army helicopter crewman.

The following information concerns the four gunship crewmen killed in action in the Ia Drang Valley on November 16, 1965, while supporting the ground forces of the 3rd Brigade, 1st Cavalry Division (Airmobile):

Warrant Officer 1 Billy J. Talley, age 27, born May 31, 1938. Hometown: McCrory, Arkansas; 8 years' service. Vietnam Wall Panel 03E, Line 67. Buried at Military Cemetery, Fort Lewis, WA.

Warrant Officer 1 Benedicto P. Bayron, age 31, born June 3, 1934. Hometown: Walanae, Hawaii; 12 years' service. Vietnam Wall Panel 03E, Line 64.

Sergeant James L. Riley, age 30, born May 8, 1935. Hometown: Vienna, West Virginia; 12 years' service. Vietnam Wall Panel 03E, Line 67.

SP5 Billy M. Knight, age 28, born September 18, 1937. Hometown: Ganado, Arizona; 10 years' service. Vietnam Wall Panel 03E, Line 66.

CHAPTER ONE

High School Warriors

Mike

I didn't know it when I woke up that morning, but my life would change drastically on August 17, 1964.

Like many American teenagers, I had always wanted to be a soldier or a Marine. After all, we were raised on a diet of John Wayne war movies and Hershey bars back then, basic elements of soldiers at war. War, however, was not on my mind when I enlisted into the United States Army. I knew nothing about Vietnam. It wasn't the big story in 1964. I did not know that Americans were risking their lives in that far away jungle nation. All I knew about the Army was what my older brother George told me about his service in Germany and the weekend visits from my history teacher, Mr. Healey, who was a sergeant in the Army National Guard.

Healey was a tall, lanky ex-marine with a crew cut who would come through our city neighborhood on the weekends in an Army Jeep with a couple of big national guardsmen. They were looking for some of our neighborhood friends who had "skipped out" of their weekend duty with the 101st Infantry Regiment. We used to call them "High School Warriors," because many of them were juniors and seniors at our school: Rindge Technical High School in Cambridge, Massachusetts, just a few city blocks from the world-famous Harvard University.

The scene was almost always the same. Mr. Healey would pull up to our street corner and ask us if we had seen his men. Of course, we told him we hadn't, and of course, he knew we were lying. Frustrated, he would speed away to continue searching all the side streets and the local ballpark for his High School Warriors. We knew his search would be fruitless. The High School Warriors had come by earlier with a hot rod Ford, hauling a small motorboat and fishing gear. They were heading down to the Charles River to enjoy the warm afternoon on the water, fishing and drinking cold beers. On Monday in history class, Mr. Healey always asked me if I had seen his men. And again, I said no. As far as I knew, he never caught any of his missing men.

★ ★ ★

After graduation in June of 1964, I was working as a stock boy in a Boston factory for $1.25 an hour. When the opportunity to enlist in the Army National Guard presented itself, I decided that it was for me. *How hard could it be? The boys could always go fishing when they wanted to, and they still got paid by the National Guard. And besides, they give you a cool looking military uniform and they wear those flat topped "Fidel Castro" hats...* I wanted one of those Castro hats, so I asked my good friend Henry to join up with me on the buddy plan.

Back then, almost half of our city neighborhood guys were in the National Guard. Before Vietnam, it was kind of a local tradition for a guy to sign up to be with his friends when he turned 17. We didn't see it as avoiding the draft, that wasn't even really a thing yet. Uncles, cousins, school buddies, and neighbors became weekend riflemen, cooks, and truck drivers. And some became "ghosts," like Mr. Healey's missing men. On a typical weekend, about ten guys would be waiting on the corner of Hurley Street for the Army Guard M211 "deuce and a half" cargo trucks to pick them up. Back then, many guys did not own cars, so the Guard sent out trucks to pick them up.

The men loaded up on the back of the trucks and their women would give them a sweet send-off. I still remember how the big trucks would belch black smoke as they pulled up the street to the cheers of their womenfolk. In the summer, the send-off was an extra special treat to witness as the Guardsmen deployed for their annual two weeks of training up in the woods of Camp Drum, New York. The sound of the trucks, the sight of their women kissing and hugging them, and the way they looked in their uniforms was enough to recruit any young, red blooded neighborhood kid. We thought that the Guard was a good deal.

It was a hot and humid August morning when I got ready to go see the National Guard recruiter. As I was leaving the house, my brother George intercepted me.

"Where you going?"

"I'm on the way to join the Guard with Henry." I puffed up proudly and then turned to leave again.

George looked at me in disbelief. "Are you crazy? The Guard is a waste of time. If you are going to join up, you should go into the Regular Army, not the National Guard."

"Why?"

"You won't see Germany and meet beautiful women and drink good German beer in the National Guard, that's why!"

After a few minutes listening to his accounts of his recent Army duty in West Germany, I began to give this Regular Army thing some thought. Traveling to a foreign country to meet beautiful women and drink good beer was very appealing. I got on the phone and called Henry to ask him if he would join the Army with me.

"What? I'll go into the National Guard with you but forget that Army stuff. Three years is too long for me." Then he hung up.

On August 13, 1964, I took the Green Line train from Lechmere Station in East Cambridge to downtown Boston to see the Army recruiter. After taking all the aptitude tests, I signed up for the aircraft repair technician course. To qualify for the course, I had to leave within three days to start basic training. On August 17, I said goodbye to my family and went to the Armed Forces Induction Center at the Boston Army Base on Summer Street. There, I raised my right hand and was sworn into the United States Army. The fun, travels, and adventures were about to begin. My only regret was that I would never receive one of those cool-looking Castro hats like Mr. Healey wore.

CHAPTER TWO

Basic Combat Training

Mike

The humid midnight air of Columbia, South Carolina was filled with the smell of barbecue chicken and diesel exhaust. The heat was oppressive for this Yankee boy. I had never been outside of Boston before, and the land of "Dixie" was a strange new world to me. I was only 18 and dumber than a block of wood. I had no idea of what life was like in other parts of the country.

I wasn't prepared at all for the scenes of stark poverty that I would see on the bus ride from the airport. Miles of country roads were lined with shanty homes between the fields of crops, housing poor people, White and Black, living on the fringes of destitution. It was a real eye opener for a young boy from the city. Back then, the civil rights movement was just taking root in the South, but I would soon find myself right in the middle of it.

Our passenger bus, loaded with new recruits for the Fort Jackson Basic Training Center, sat in the parking lot of a rundown 1950s bus depot out in the Carolina countryside. Bright-yellow neon lights glowed in the darkness, reflecting off the side windows of the bus as we looked out to see a surreal scene of elderly Black couples, middle-aged White farmers, and teenage mothers with small children walking in and out of a small cafeteria. When we got off the bus and went inside for a cold soda, we stood around taking in the sights of all these night travelers eating hot corndogs and drinking Doctor Pepper colas.

We weren't expecting the separate restrooms for travelers. There were restrooms for "Negroes Only" and restrooms for "Whites Only." Back in

Boston, we all used the same restrooms. This was our first introduction to the Deep South.

The bus drivers mingled in front of the dispatch office, chain smoking cigarettes and drinking cups of coffee to keep them awake for the long drive ahead. After a fifteen-minute stay, we loaded back onto our bus and settled in for the next adventure. For most of us new recruits, encountering the bus depot and the sights and strange new smells from down in the land of Dixie was a powerful experience that we would always remember. As our bus pulled out of the depot, we found ourselves wondering what our next experience would be, somewhere out in that dark Southern night.

Our military escort was supposed to have met us at the Columbia Airport when our plane landed from Boston, but he was a no show. Lucky for us, the driver was waiting outside the airport terminal to pick us up. As we left the bus depot, our driver advised us that we would be going downtown to pick up the sergeant. A few miles down the highway, we reached the outskirts of downtown Columbia and rolled to a stop in front of a honky-tonk bar. The driver parked the bus and went inside to find our escort. Those of us who were still awake peered out the windows to watch the action. The streets were empty, with patches of dim light dotting the sidewalks. The bar was alive, and the sound of country music flowed from its open door. The sight of dancing bodies framed the doorway.

After a few minutes, the driver came out of the swirling smoke and sounds, arm in arm with a soldier. They slowly stumbled up the stairs of the bus and the soldier fell into a front seat. He turned and looked at us with glassy eyes. Then he began to curse and shout at us. "Listen up, you bunch of maggots! I'm Sergeant Lester and I'm in charge here. You got that?"

"Yes sir!"

His glare made it immediately obvious that our response had been unacceptable to him. A hush settled upon the rows of sleepy-eyed young men. The sergeant threw out some more curses while the driver put the bus in gear and drove off towards the Army post. As the bus rolled down the road, Sergeant Lester stood up, swaying back and forth with the movement of the bus, his drunken legs just barely supporting his weight.

"What the hell kind of answer is that? I want to hear you people, do you understand?"

This time we gave the man what he wanted, a loud yell that reverberated through the bus.

"YES SIR!"

"That's better." A brief smile passed over his lips. "But from now on, you don't call sergeants 'sir.' I ain't no officer, you got that?"

"YES SERGEANT!"

Sergeant Lester dropped back into his seat, lit up a cigarette, and began to give the driver directions to the Army post. As they argued over the correct road to take, we were glad to be out from under his attention, even if it was for just a few moments. We sat in our seats wondering what our fate would be. Some of us were deep in thought, others were deep in sleep. We would soon discover that sleep and deep thought would be in limited supply during our basic training. Sergeant Lester would be the first in a long line of Army NCOs who would be on our backs for the next eight weeks as we converted from soft, undisciplined civilians into a platoon of motivated soldiers.

After riding for about a half hour, we arrived at the reception station at Fort Jackson. The sergeant staggered off the bus and stood by the open door. He pulled out a piece of paper from his jacket and tried to read off our names as we filed out of the bus. But it was too dark, and he was too drunk to read the list. He eventually gave up and snapped at us to hurry up. We scurried down the narrow aisle and out the door. He made us form up into two columns and began to give us a little lecture.

"You men are in for it! If you expect to make it out of here, you better keep your mouths shut and your heads out of your asses. I don't care if you were a football jock or a city punk. You don't know what it means to be tough. In the next few weeks, you're gonna find out what tough really means. Now get down on your bellies and give me twenty push-ups!"

He was still drunk, but his bark was loud. We fell to the ground and slowly began to go through the motions of doing push-ups. As we grunted and strained, he got back on the bus and shouted from the doorway as it roared out of the parking lot.

"Stay right where you are and keep them push-ups going! Someone will be here to get you!"

As the smell and dust of the bus exhaust blew in our faces and we watched the taillights disappear into the darkness, our push-ups came to an abrupt stop. Suddenly, it was dead quiet. We lingered around wondering what was going to happen next. Two am turned to three am, and it began to get chilly and damp.

Off to one side of the lot was a streetlight and a one-story wood building with a wide staircase. We decided to go over and sit on the stairs while awaiting our fate. By now, we were exhausted from our long ordeal, and we huddled together, trying to keep warm. We waited and waited but no one came to meet us. At some point, lights began to come on in the buildings along the road, and soon we heard noise. In the distance we could hear, but not see, men yelling and heavy footsteps. The sound grew louder and closer with each passing moment. Soon they were upon us, hundreds of men in white T-shirts, running along the dark streets, shouting in cadence while their boots hit the pavement in a steady, beating rhythm. Although mesmerized by the base coming to life, we were tired and hungry, not having slept or eaten since the previous day. As the sun came up over a hazy horizon, we were still waiting. Finally, round about 6am, a lone soldier walked up to us and instructed us to pick up our bags and follow him.

He took us to a mess hall for breakfast and hot coffee and then we were marched to a row of administrative buildings where we were processed in. From there, he led us to a barber shop where they cut off our hair. Next came a big warehouse where we lined up for uniform issue. After receiving a duffle bag filled with fresh new Army clothes, we were taken to a row of old World War II wooden barracks and assigned a bunkbed and a wall locker.

For the remainder of the day, we were told to clean up the barracks for inspection. After sweeping and washing the floors and the bathroom, which was called a "latrine," we stood by our bunks waiting for a sergeant to inspect our work. But when he entered our barracks, he did not bother to inspect anything. Instead, he called out our names and told us we would be pulling a thing called "fire watch" during the night. Fire watch consisted of a one-hour duty where we had to walk around outside the barracks with a red helmet liner and a flashlight and keep an eye out for fire in and around the barracks. After the evening meal, we waited sleepily in our barracks to start our assigned duty.

My watch was from 1am to 2am. As I sat on my bunk waiting to serve my time, I reflected on the events of the past thirty or so hours and concluded that the Army was a nightmare. I couldn't believe that I had enlisted for three years. Once I pulled my duty of fire watch, I climbed into my bunk and immediately fell into a deep sleep. The few hours of sleep I got was a luxury and by the next morning, at 0430 hours Army time, the manic routine continued.

Each day at the reception station was worse than the day before. Sergeants constantly yelled at us, making us do endless push-ups when we were too slow, and regular details called "police call," picking up trash and cigarettes. Finally, on the third day, a sergeant came with news of relief.

"Men, you will soon be leaving this area for your training companies. This place will be behind you as you move on to Tank Hill, where life won't be so bad anymore."

Knowing that we would soon be leaving the reception station that we called the "Hell Hole" was some comfort to us. While waiting for the trucks that would transport us to arrive, we wondered what this place called "Tank Hill" was. By mid-afternoon we were on our way. The Army cargo trucks carried us past rows and rows of white wooden barracks, up a steep hill towards our new home. Our eyes scanned the top of the hill for signs of armored vehicles (tanks), but we saw none. *Why was it called Tank Hill?*

When we arrived at our new company, we found out. There were no Army tanks on the hill. The "tank" was a large water reservoir tank which was used as a reference point by soldiers when they were out in the field on long marches.

The trucks parked, and we unloaded our duffle bags and lined up in the street in front of the orderly and supply room buildings. A tall, muscular sergeant came out of the orderly room in a freshly pressed fatigue uniform with large sergeant first class stripes on his sleeves. He began to pace up and down the rows of recruits, stopping to look a few of us in the face. Then he stood in the center of our formation and introduced himself.

"I am Sergeant Lynn. I will be your senior training NCO while you are here at Delta Company. The Army wants me to make you all into good soldiers. God help us. You will learn that there are no individuals here, only team players. You Are Now Delta Team!"

Sergeant Lynn then called a group of his NCOs to the front and had our group broken down into platoons. Each platoon was given to one of the NCOs for them to take charge of our training. We were lucky in my platoon, for we got a nice, mild-mannered NONCOM (non-commissioned officer) named Sergeant Ward. Sergeant Ward was a short, thin, Black man who spoke softly to us, like an uncle. He was about 30 years old at the time, and was married, living off base. He would soon be putting in long hours of day and night work, trying to mold us into fighting men.

After the assignments, Sergeant Ward led us over to our barracks and got us settled in. Each man was assigned a bunk bed, wall locker, and footlocker. This building would be our home for the next eight weeks. We spent that first night getting the barracks cleaned and polished, the first night of a regular routine that would be part of our training.

Our training got underway immediately. We had daily physical training, running a few miles in our combat boots every morning at 0600 hours, swinging through ladder bars before going to breakfast chow, long days of learning about our M-14 rifles, practicing on the bayonet range, and 10-mile marches out to the rifle ranges for marksmanship training. It seemed every moment of the day was filled with some kind of Army training. In the evening, we would clean and secure our weapons and equipment and proceed to the mess hall for chow. We were always hungry after burning up so many calories throughout the day. The final meal of the day was especially important, as it was the last food we got until the morning. There were no snacks allowed in basic training.

One evening, I was standing in front of the mess hall waiting for my turn to enter the building. While waiting, we had to stand at parade rest four feet apart from each other and read the general orders which were printed on small signs attached to the side of the mess hall. As I studied my general orders, I got an unexpected visit from Sergeant Lynn. He was walking along the line of recruits weeding out anyone he felt was out of order, such as a man with unpolished boots or improper dress. Suddenly, he came up behind me and called me out of line. I came to attention and made an about face. He leaned forward and put his nose close to my face.

"Boy, when was the last time you had a haircut?"

"Sergeant, I had one three days ago."

"You're a damn liar, recruit! Get your ass out of this line and get up to the barber shop now!"

I quickly fell out of the chow line and ran up the hill to the barber shop. I got in line and waited my turn, all the while watching the wall clock as it ticked towards closing time for the chow hall. I got my haircut and ran as fast as I could back to the mess hall as soon as they finished. But it was closed. I had missed chow and was one hungry recruit that night. I vowed then and there that I would never again get on Sergeant Lynn's shit list. In his own cruel way, he had shown me the meaning of keeping myself straight. I took extra effort to always look my best from then on.

I was lucky that I had not received Sergeant Lynn's "special treatment." When he saw a recruit messing up, he would make them do 25 push-ups, followed by a run through the ladder bars, and a low crawl. Sergeant Lynn had a knack for remembering names, and he would harass anyone he felt was a screw up. I avoided him at all costs during my time on Tank Hill.

As I began to adjust to my new Army life, I began to meet a few new friends to talk with. One of those new friends was a farm kid from Mississippi named Johnson. Johnson was a big boy accustomed to heavy fieldwork on his grandmother's farm, and he often told me how religious his family was. He told me that I was the first White boy he ever was friendly with. When I asked him why, he told me about what life was like in the segregated South. It was all new to me. As I said before, when I was growing up, segregation wasn't really a thing I was exposed to.

It wasn't long before our friendship was put to the test. A few weeks into our training, we were both on latrine cleanup duty. As we washed out the sinks, two Negro city guys from another squad came into the latrine and called Johnson over to them. They spoke as though I wasn't even there, telling him that they did not want him getting friendly with me. One of them called him an "Uncle Tom." I kept scrubbing the sink trying to mind my own business. Finally, they left, and Johnson returned to his duties with me. His eyes were filled with sadness.

"What were they talking about?"

"I ain't supposed to be talking with you White boys."

"Why not? What's the problem with talking?"

"You don't understand, do you? Down here we are not allowed to have White friends, understand?"

"Ya, sure. I guess."

But I really didn't understand what he meant. In my high school, White kids and Black kids got along fairly well. Back then, I never had a problem with race relations. I just did not get this new set up. In the weeks to come, I got to see how all the Southern boys disliked my friendship with Johnson.

"Kelley, don't get too friendly with that Black boy if you know what's good for you. Yer lookin' for trouble."

Now, I not only had a few Black guys unhappy about me and Johnson, but the White guys were not happy either. It seemed our friendship was doomed. Once we understood the situation, Johnson and I began to keep our distance from each other. This was my first experience with Southern segregation, and I did not like it.

Until my last week of basic training, I tried to keep a low profile. It was not easy. Occasionally, Johnson and I threw a friendly nod to each other. That was it. No talking anymore. In our last days in the platoon before graduation day, Johnson came over to me and shook my hand.

"Soldier boy, you're a good guy! Don't let them change you."

That was the last I ever saw of Johnson, but as the months and years went by, I met others like him. I also met many men who, whether Black or White, drew invisible lines in the sand that made it difficult for me and the Johnsons of the world to form relationships. The sixties were a time of unrest and turmoil in American society, and it found its way into the military.

Despite the hardships and difficulties of basic training, I survived. All the forced marches with full field packs were over. All the long days firing on the ranges and running until you felt your lungs would burst were now behind us. The Army had made us into soldiers. I was now looking forward to my next assignment at the Army Aviation School.

CHAPTER THREE

Helicopter School

Mike

After a long, cross-country bus ride through the Deep South, we arrived at Fort Rucker, Alabama, home of the U.S. Army's Aviation School Training Center near the city of Dothan. I was excited about my new duty assignment. The lessons I learned in basic training had prepared me for this next experience in the land of Dixie. The bus pulled into the parking lot of the Enlisted Student Center and we got off and formed up in a small platoon to wait for our NCO.

We were processed in to the school and given an old World War II barracks to live in. I was assigned to the first floor, and my new squad leader was a guy named Specialist Henry, who had re-enlisted in the Army to get a chance to attend the aviation school. He was a tall, lanky, good-natured fellow who took the time to show us young soldiers the ways of Army life. In the weeks to come, Henry would be our unofficial "uncle."

The school would be a big change for us. It was a more laid-back routine, with no sergeants yelling in our faces. It was almost like a civilian job. We attended classes from 0730 hours until 1630 hours, and had the evenings and weekends off duty. In between going to aviation classes, some of us had to pull kitchen police duty (KP) at the mess hall, usually on a weekend, where we spent all day washing dishes, pots and pans, and mopping floors. Our free time was spent drinking cheap beer at the snack bar or going to see a movie for 25 cents. Occasionally they would give us a pass to go off base. The closest big town was Dothan, about a half-hour ride down the main highway.

Shortly after our arrival, on a mild November afternoon, my new buddy Joe Aragona from Massapequa, New York, and I began to hitchhike our way to Dothan to explore life outside the Army post.

The first leg of our trip was courtesy of an off-post sergeant who gave us a lift in his pickup truck from the main gate out to the highway. From there, we walked a few miles along the road with our thumbs up for a ride. Several cars sped right by us, and it looked as though we would not get a ride to Dothan.

Then, an old, beat up 1952 Ford Sedan pulled over to the side of the road and the driver waved at us. We quickly ran to the car and looked inside to see an elderly Black couple.

"Where are you boys going?"

"We're trying to get to Dothan." I pointed down the road in the direction we were headed.

"Well, I'm going through there if you want a ride. You can get in the back there."

Joe and I glanced at each other, briefly wondering if we should accept the ride. One look down the long highway was enough to make up our minds.

"Thank you." We climbed into the back seat of the old car. The car rolled slowly along the right lane of the highway.

"Where you boys from?"

"He's from New York, and I came down from Boston."

"That's quite a trip. What do you think of things down here in Alabama so far?"

We glanced at each other, not knowing what to say without bringing up the strained race relations that were the biggest difference between home and the South that we had noticed, and possibly offending him.

"Well," Joe said, "we're really very new to the area and haven't seen anything yet."

That seemed to satisfy them, and we engaged in small talk for the rest of the ride. From what we could tell, they were on their way to a market to buy food and visit their grandchildren. From the broken seat, a coil spring stuck out under my leg and pinched me, and the seats were so worn that the stuffing was coming out of them. Just two blocks from the downtown district, the old man pulled the Ford over to the side of the road and turned to look at us with sad eyes.

"Sorry I got to do this, boys. But we can't drive no White boys downtown, understand?"

"That's okay. We can walk the rest of the way. Thanks for the ride."

As the old couple drove off, we began to walk towards the main drag a few blocks away. Across the street from where we got out of the car was a small wooden home with some people sitting on chairs on the front porch. It wasn't long after the old couple's car disappeared down the street when some teenage boys and a couple of men came out and stood on the porch, looking our way. We began to feel uncomfortable. We figured they had seen us getting out of the Ford and knew that we were in trouble. At that instant, we both got the urge to run for it and we ran the two blocks in rapid time. Our drill instructors from basic training would have been proud of us. All those brutal morning runs at Fort Jackson had paid off. We made it to the safety of the main street. This was our first experience with the local no-mixing rules of Dixieland.

After catching our breath and composure, we began to walk along Main Street to take in the sights. Dothan was a small, sleepy city. The main attraction was the Five and Dime department store. Joe and I went inside, sat down at the lunch counter, and ordered their special apple peach pie at the Whites-only section. Afterwards, we walked down to the big Peanut Festival we heard was happening on the outskirts of Main Street. There, we saw segregated bathrooms with hand painted signs denoting which bathrooms were for "Whites Only" and which were for "Colored Only." This continued to be a cultural difference that I would struggle to accustom myself to.

I saw a hot dog stand and bought a hot dog that was unlike any hot dog I had ever had before. I remembered seeing them at the bus depot, and I was curious. It was called a corn dog and came on a stick, not in a hot dog roll like those we had up North. They had large jars of mustard to dip the dog in before you ate it. I took a bite and right away I did not like the taste of it, so I tossed it away. Within seconds, two small Black boys in torn clothes picked it up, wiped it off, and ate it.

Joe and I looked at each other in disbelief. So, this is Dixieland. That night, we stayed in a run-down flop house that they called a hotel. The next morning, we ate breakfast in a local café. The juke box was playing "Mr. Lonely" by Bobby Vinton and it made me homesick. I was a long way from home and my foray into the civilian world reminded me of that fact in a way that I hadn't had the time to think about during training.

After breakfast, we began our long journey back to the Army post. There was no bus to ride to the base, so we had to hitch a ride or walk. We spent the morning on the edge of the city, trying to hitch a ride, but no one stopped. We were running out of time to get back, so we walked out of the city and into the countryside, full of open fields of crops and farms.

As we walked, and the sun came out, it got hot and we became very thirsty. It was a good thing we had been conditioned by the Army for long marches in the boondocks, for if we had been the soft civilians we were just a few short months before, we would have been in bad shape. At one point, we came upon a small gas station and bought a bottle of cold soda to soothe our dry throats, which helped a little.

As we continued to walk along the deserted farm road to the base, we looked up in the sky to see Huey helicopters flying over our heads.

"Don't you wish we could signal them? You think they would come down to rescue us?" Joe looked up at the helicopters longingly.

"Yes, they could bring us back to base." Of course, we both realized that wasn't a realistic possibility.

By late afternoon, we made it to the main gate.

"Whoa, you boys been in a fight or something?" the military policeman (MP) at the gate asked us as he let us in. We just looked at him wearily as we continued our trek. It was still a mile or so to go before we would reach our barracks and we were exhausted. Just then, a soldier pulled up in his truck and offered us a ride to post. We were so relieved.

To this day, I still remember how good the shower felt on my overheated body. I must have stood under the running water for 15 minutes to cool off. Even the evening meal at the mess hall tasted like Texas steak.

Fort Rucker never looked so good to us.

On Monday it was back to school. Hitting the books, studying all the technical materials, and going into the shops for some hands-on mechanical training. That was the best part of the school, working on aircraft engines and sub-systems. We got to use all the special tools and repair real airplanes. I loved it.

One day, early in my training, they took us out to the airfield to go for a ride in a Bell OH-13 observation helicopter. I had never been in a helicopter before, and when the pilot took off and climbed into the sky my stomach felt like it was in my chest. I didn't know it at the time, but soon I would be flying helicopters as part of my job.

As the weeks went by, more and more students arrived at the aviation school. Some of them wore an unusual shoulder patch, a blue and white insignia with wings and the number 11 set in the center. Specialist Henry told us they were from a unit up in Fort Benning, Georgia called the 11th Air Assault Division. They had come down to Fort Rucker to get some cross training in aviation, along with some advanced training on the Bell UH-1 Huey.

On coffee breaks, we got to talk with some of the 11th Air Assault guys and they told us about a large, simulated wargame they had just completed up in the Carolinas.

"I remember seeing a lot of Hueys flying low level out over the pine woods of Fort Jackson when I was in basic in August of 1964."

"That was our unit," one of the guys confirmed my thoughts.

This special unit was the basis for a new type of Army division called the Air Cavalry that was especially trained for jungle warfare in Vietnam. But in December of 1964, I had no visions of a place called Vietnam. The only time I heard about it was when one of our instructors would tell us about flying and repairing helicopters there. My sights were set on going to Germany, meeting pretty fräuleins and drinking lots of good German beer, just like my brother had. He told me they had helicopters in Germany, and that was where I wanted to go. As far as I was concerned, the fun, travel, and adventures were just a few months away. As soon as my training was completed, I would be shipped to Germany, and I would live the life of Elvis Presley in the movie G.I. Blues. It was Germany or bust!

Just before Christmas, the Army allowed us to take leave to go home for the holidays. I had not been home since I enlisted in August, and I was looking forward to seeing my family and friends. One of the older soldiers in our barracks owned a car and he offered to drive people to New York City for $35. I was able to join a group of four students that would travel in his car. We packed our bags into the trunk of the soldier's 1961 Ford Sedan and departed Fort Rucker a few days before Christmas.

As we drove through Southern Georgia, we decided to stop at a roadside café to eat. We were just sitting for a few moments before the waitress came over.

"Hi boys, how you doing?" She smiled uncomfortably. "Look, I hate to say this, but I can't serve one of you."

One of our passengers was a Black soldier from New York City. "That's okay," he said. "I can go out and wait in the car so the rest of you can eat." He started to get up when the soldier who was driving us stopped him.

"No. You have as much of a right to eat as any of us. You're not waiting in the car."

The waitress shifted uncomfortably on her feet before she went to the back of the café to talk to the cook, a large man in his mid-50s. He came over to our table.

"Listen boys, I don't want no trouble with you. If your boy will go out to the back door, I will give him some food. The rest of you I can feed at the table. If I feed the boy here, I will get into big trouble, do you understand?"

The driver looked at the rest of us. "If he don't eat with us, we don't eat here."

We looked at each other and nodded in agreement. All at once, we got up and walked to the door.

"I'm real sorry I couldn't feed you boys, but if I served that boy, they would burn my place down tonight."

Right then, we realized that we were still deep in the heart of Dixieland and could not expect this poor cook to do us any favors. We got into the car and drove away, wondering when and how we would ever eat any food.

A few miles down the road, we saw a small supermarket. The driver pulled into the parking lot and had us pool our money. We sent one guy into the store to buy us some food. A few minutes later, our man returned with a bag of groceries. We got back on the road eating bologna and cheese sandwiches with potato chips as we continued up north. Our crisis had passed.

When we got to northern Virginia, we stopped at a roadside diner and went inside to eat. There, we had no problem being served. It was our first hot, cooked meal since leaving Fort Rucker. Shortly after that, we arrived at Penn Station in downtown New York City where the driver let us off curbside. I went inside and bought a ticket to Boston, and made my way home for a short leave with my family and friends.

The Army sent me to three helicopter technical courses that would last until the middle of February 1965. The first class I was with was shipped to Germany, but I was sent to another school. I spent two weeks in a holdover company awaiting my final school, pulling various dirty details, including a lot of KP at the consolidated mess hall for students.

One day while I was there, I was sent to the mess hall for the warrant officer school and got an inside look at how difficult it was for the warrant officer candidates going through their training. Their training instructors were a bunch of tough bastards who made life miserable for the candidates. Outside the mess hall, I saw them running along the sidewalks to classes. Every few minutes, a TAC officer would stop them on the street and make them do push-ups for some minor infraction. I learned later from my pilots that the cruel treatment used by the instructors was their way of weeding out the unqualified people. After watching the candidates for a while, I was grateful to be an enlisted man on KP duty.

By the time I began my final school on the CH-21 Shawnee twin-rotor cargo helicopter, the base was full of students from the 11th Air Assault Division. Rumors were circulating that all graduating students would be assigned to the new division and shipped to Vietnam. The last thing I wanted was to be assigned to the new division. My hopes and dreams were set on seeing Europe.

When I reported to Shawnee School, I met a new bunch of friends. One was a kid from California named Robert "Tommy" Warner. He was a tall, red-haired boy who liked to talk about his Honda motorcycle and the beautiful girls of his hometown of Gonzales. Every time a Beach Boys song came on the radio, he would sing along and tell us how great life was in sunny California, a place I knew nothing about before meeting Tommy. The two of us spent a lot of time hanging out with another California boy named Dave Pancoke. Tommy, Dave, and I spent a lot of time going to the bowling alley and the beer hall, swapping stories about our hometowns and girlfriends. All of us were motorheads and loved anything with wheels on it. Dave and I had built modified cars before military service and Tommy had raced his motorcycle at all the local tracks in central California. Having such good friends made my Army life much more enjoyable.

Upon graduation from Shawnee School in February 1965, we received our orders for our first duty assignment. Almost the whole class was sent to Davison Army Airfield at Fort Belvoir, Virginia, just outside Washington, D.C. We were all excited about our orders, and eager to get to work on the fleet of Army helicopters at Davison Airfield. We cleaned out our wall lockers and packed our bags for the trip to the nation's capital. We were given travel pay and an airline ticket, and then signed out of our student company. We were now trained and qualified to be aviation mechanics.

We took a taxi to the small Dothan Municipal Airport where we caught a flight on Southern Airways up to Atlanta International Airport for our main flight to Washington, D.C. As we rode along the dark Alabama highway, I looked out the windows and saw the shadows of farms passing in the night and remembered my experiences in the land of Dixie. It was good to be moving on.

HEADQUARTERS

U.S. ARMY AVIATION CENTER TROOP BRIGADE (Prov)

Fort Rucker, Alabama 36362

SPECIAL ORDERS 12 February 1965

NUMBER 21 EXTRACT

21.TC 221. Fol reg dir. WF TDN. 2152010 01-1151 P 1411 s99-999.

Rel Asg: Enl Stu Co (Stu) USAAVNS Regt (3186)

Ft. Rucker, Ala

Asg to: 3rd TC Co (Lt Hcptr) Ft. Belvoir, Va.

Rpt date: 21 Feb 65

Sp Instr: EM will not depart this station prior to 1500 hrs

19 Feb 65

SMITH, DAVID O Pvt E-2

WARNER, ROBERT T Pvt E-2

PANCOKE, DAVID L. Pvt E-2

THORHILL, MICHAEL E Pvt E-2

KELLEY, MICHAEL L. Pvt E-2

HILTON, DANNY L Pvt E-2

BOTKIN, ROBERT L Pvt E-2

FOR THE COMMANDER:

OFFICIAL: LA VERT W. JONES

JACK D. WATERS 1st LT, INF

CWO W-2, USA Adjutant

Asst Adjutant

CHAPTER FOUR

Flying Shawnee Bananas

Mike

We arrived in Washington, D.C. on a very cold February afternoon. An Army 2½ ton cargo truck picked us up at the airport terminal. We loaded our baggage and climbed into the truck for the freezing ride out to Fort Belvoir, which was about ten miles west of the airport. Upon arrival at the base, we reported into the orderly room of the 3rd Transportation Company (Light Helicopter), a CH-21 Shawnee unit. We were assigned billets in one of the many World War II barracks that lined the streets. These barracks were much more comfortable than the ones we lived in at Fort Rucker. The first floor had a pool room, and a TV room with soda machines, and the second floor was a large open bay lined with modern, gray double bunk beds. The company mess hall was a short walk down the sidewalk, and one block over was the Service Club and post theater. A civilian transit bus stop was nearby, in the event you wanted to go downtown to visit the nation's capital.

Within a few days, we were sent down to Davison Army Airfield to work on the big CH-21 Shawnee cargo helicopters. These helicopters were nicknamed "Flying Bananas" because the fuselage was long, and it had a curve in the middle like a banana. These big birds had large twin rotors with a tri-cycle landing gear. They were built during the 1950s, and by the time I was flying them they were at the end of their service life in the Army.

Many of the aircraft on the flight line had flown in Vietnam, and we would examine the sheet metal patches where they had taken hits from enemy ground fire during their time in combat from 1961 to 1964.

We were assigned to a repair maintenance crew and issued new Army aviation toolboxes. On my first day working on a CH-21, I looked around the hangar and watched the beehive of aviation activity. There were technicians installing main rotors, mechanics working on sub-systems like fuel and hydraulics, and ground crews moving aircraft in and out of the hangar. It was very busy.

Outside, I could hear the rumble of engines as test pilots fired up their machines for a pre-flight check and helicopters flew overhead. *I am a lucky soldier to be part of this important operation.* The recruiter in Boston had told me I would get to work on Army aircraft, and he sure kept his promise. Being in Army Aviation was exciting stuff for a 19-year-old kid. But the best was yet to come.

On Fridays, we knocked off work, rolled the helicopters outside to the tarmac, and cleaned out the hangar. We swept and washed the floors and then, at about 1600 hours, the mess hall sent a truck full of sandwiches and food to the hangar and set up tables to place the food on. A sergeant would show up with his pickup truck and on the back of the truck was a couple of cold kegs of beer. We would all have something to eat, and drink beer. This was called a company party and us new guys really enjoyed this special treat.

After a few hours, the duty truck would pick us up and drive us back to the barracks. From there we were off duty. We would take a shower, put on some civilian clothes, and head down to the nightclubs on 14th Street in Washington, D.C. The nightlife of the nation's capital was a great experience for a young man. They had "go-go" bars where they would play all the hit songs of 1965 while beautiful girls danced in cages that hung from the ceiling. We could sit for hours drinking large pitchers of beer for $2.00, eating bowls of popcorn and potato chips.

My buddies Tommy and Dave had dated college girls before they had enlisted, and one night we decided to go "uptown" to visit the nightclubs in the Georgetown neighborhood where a lot of college girls hung out. We went into one club and began talking to a group of pretty girls. Tommy and Dave moved over to engage a few of them in conversation, and left me with a few girls of my own to talk to. I soon found myself out of my class, however, and realized my high school education did not match the intellectual level required to sustain a conversation with these educated ladies. To my delight, my buddies noticed me struggling to talk with the girls and soon returned to my side.

"How's it going, Kelley?"

"Not so good. I'm outta my class here."

"That's alright." Dave offered a reassuring smile. "We can go back to 14th Street for a few more beers."

It was a warm spring evening, and we decided to walk around downtown after leaving the bars. We arrived at the gates of the White House and looked up to the lighted windows, fascinated that we were this close to President Lyndon B. Johnson. Little did we know that in that White House, LBJ and his advisors were planning our future.

We caught the last bus back to the post and were hungry when we arrived, so we went over to our company mess hall to see if we could get something to eat. Lucky for us, our mess hall was responsible for feeding all military policemen on night duty, so when we got there at about midnight, they were open for business and made us some sandwiches. It was just another nice perk we had at our new unit of assignment, and such a difference from where I had been before. The mess hall always served great food and had such good Army cooks.

We arrived back at our barracks and many of the guys were still up hanging around and talking. I remember one guy from that night. He was a regular winner of the post commander's "Soldier of the Month" award.

"Hey, man. How is it that you're able to beat everyone out in the competition like you do all the time?"

He shrugged. "Probably just my past experience. I used to be a part of the 3rd Infantry from the Tomb of the Unknown Soldier over at Fort Myers."

"The Old Guard?"

"Yeah."

"Oh man. Could you show us some of your moves?"

He went over to his wall locker and retrieved a highly polished pair of black, low quarter Army shoes and took them into the latrine. In a moment, he came out, dressed in a T-shirt and a pair of boxer shorts, wearing his special Army shoes. Each shoe had metal tabs grafted into the heels and toes which made a clicking sound when he walked. He came to attention at the entrance of the squad bay, holding a broom as a rifle. Then, he began a smart slow walk down the middle of the bay. When he reached the end, he stopped, spun the broom around like a color guard drill team, brought it to port arms, and made an about face, clicking his heels with the movements. Then he came back down the bay, repeating his moves. We all sat in awe of this fine soldier.

As the weeks went by and we gained more and more work experience on the aircraft, we began to go out on test flights. When a bird had been overhauled in the maintenance hangar, a test pilot and co-pilot would have to take the aircraft up for a test flight to see if it was in flying condition before it could be returned to the fleet for operational missions. My buddies Tommy and Dave would always volunteer to go on these "check" rides, and most of the time I would join them. All we had to do was get permission from our group leader and an okay from the senior sergeant first class maintenance supervisor to pick up a flight helmet from supply and board the aircraft. We had 25 CH-21s, 5 CH-34s and 2 OH-13s in our unit, so there was always a bird scheduled for a test flight.

Some of the Shawnees were specially equipped with luxury passenger seats for flying high ranking officers around the Washington, D.C. area, especially for trips over to the Pentagon. These birds were called V.I.P. aircraft. Davison Army Airfield was a major transportation center for flying military brass. In addition to the cargo and V.I.P. aircraft, we always had one CH-21 on a 24-hour Red Alert standby next to the flight operations building. If they received a Red Alert notification, the crews would scramble to the aircraft, get the engine up to maximum power, and get airborne as quickly as possible. Watching the crews drill for a Red Alert was always a treat. Despite the fact these old birds were almost obsolete, they were still an impressive sight to watch when they were in motion.

Our pilots had a special love for them as many of them had flown the Flying Bananas in combat over jungles, rugged mountains, and across the vast delta of South Vietnam. They were ugly looking aircraft, but we soon took a liking to these beasts of burden. The battle-tested old birds had survived hundreds of dangerous missions and were now flying on easy stateside duty as war veterans. Going up on a check ride was always a lot of fun and excitement.

A typical flight consisted of two pilots (an aircraft commander and a co-pilot) and a crew chief. When we went up on a check flight, we always helped the crew chief get the bird ready to go. It took a lot to get the CH-21 into the air; it was a lazy aircraft. When the pilots would fire up the R-1820 radial engine, it would cough, sputter, backfire, and blow out flumes of smoke like a World War II bomber. When they cranked up the RPMs, the twin rotors would engage and begin to slowly turn like a windmill. Once the engine bay was checked for fires and leaks, the crew chief had to run to the front of the aircraft and give a "thumbs up" signal to the pilots to show all systems were good to go. Then he would pull out the wheel chocks and climb inside the cargo bay.

On our rides, we also climbed in and sat in either a V.I.P. seat or on a regular canvas troop seat. The old bird would roar like a lion as the pilots brought up the power for a magneto check. Once all the pre-flight checks were completed, the pilots would release the brakes and begin a slow taxi down the flight line and over to the active runway to await clearance from the control tower. As it taxied out to the ramp, its vintage engine sounded like a freight train on full throttle. The aircraft swayed back and forth like a slow-moving elephant, and above our heads, the long center drive shafts whined like a banshee. We had to wear special ear protectors because the noise was so loud. Everything that could vibrate, vibrated.

The CH-21 could lift straight up, nose over, and take off like any helicopter, but this transitional flight was a stress on the old warbirds, so our pilots always made what they called a running takeoff. The pilots sat in the cockpit next to each other, like in a World War II bomber. The crew chief switched from side to side, looking out the open doors and making sure the aircraft was clear on both sides. At the end of the ramp, the pilot would call the tower for permission to take off.

"Davison Tower, this is Army 227 ready for takeoff!"

"Army 227, proceed to south end of runway. You are cleared for takeoff!"

"Roger Tower, Army 227 proceeding to south end of runway for takeoff."

The pilot looked back into the cargo bay and asked the crew chief if all was okay. The crew chief gave him the thumbs up signal. Everything was good to go. If all systems were ready, the pilot rolled up the collective control and brought the engine up to maximum takeoff RPM, then released the brakes and pushed the cyclic control, tilting the rotor blades forward for lift and speed. The big Banana bird would roll down the runway, slowly picking up speed on its three large rubber tires. When it reached take-off speed, the pilot would pull up on the collective control and "Walanda!", the old bird became airborne, lifting its two hind outboard wheels off the ground, balancing on its nose wheel for a few more feet until the wind got under her long, lazy belly and then up, up, up she went into the wide blue yonder. What a great feeling it was climbing out of Davison airspace, gaining airspeed and altitude over the majestic Potomac River and seeing the skyline of the nation's capital.

This was heady stuff for a kid who had been hanging out on a city street corner with no future plans just a year before. I was loving every minute of it. Flying and working on the CH-21 Shawnee fulfilled all the expectations I had held the day I signed my enlistment papers. The recruiting poster claimed the Army offered "Fun, Travel, and Adventure," and I was getting all these things from the Flying Banana.

On April 18, eight months after I had joined the Army, I was promoted to private first class, my very first stripe. This meant a little more money in my pocket each month. Our basic privates' pay was only $78 a month, which did not go very far, so we had to watch our spending habits. Some guys would blow their month's pay in a night of playing pool or drinking down in the clubs of 14th Street. But I saved my money, so I could go home when I had a week's leave.

On one of my trips, I booked a standby flight (hop) out of Andrews Air Force base across town and my plans were to take a transit bus over there on a Friday afternoon. One of my Shawnee pilots, a warrant officer, found out I was going to Andrews to catch a hop and he took me into our flight operations office to see the duty officer.

"Captain, PFC Kelley is going home on leave. He has a hop over at Andrews. Any problem if we fly him over there, sir?"

The duty officer looked at me and my tiny PFC stripes. "Chief, your aircraft is a V.I.P. bird. How do I justify flying a private as a V.I.P.?"

"Well sir, we think he is an important guy. He is one of our best mechanics, captain."

The duty officer looked perplexed. He scratched his head and mumbled a bit. "I could get into trouble if the commander discovered I was giving V.I.P. flights to privates, chief."

Some good-natured banter then followed between the officers, some of it sounding a little like blackmail. Then the captain gave in.

"Oh, alright then. Go and file your flight plan and get the hell out of here!"

The chief warrant officer pilot told me to rush back to my barracks and change into my Class A dress uniform. The duty driver made the round trip in good time, and we boarded the V.I.P. CH-21 and took off to the Air Force base. It was an experience I will never forget.

We landed on the large airfield and taxied up to the operations center. A small group of officers and enlisted passengers were waiting on the tarmac for the outbound flight. Our crew chief opened the side cargo door to let me out. As I strutted towards the waiting group, my pilot looked out his side window and wished me a good leave home. When I turned to wave goodbye, the old Flying Banana looked so fine in its shiny olive-green, high-gloss paint with the big white "U.S. ARMY" letters on its fuselage. I was so proud, I felt a lump in my throat. Then the aircraft taxied away with its engine roaring. As they rolled down the runway and climbed into the blue sky, the spectators were bewildered. The operations sergeant had me fill out a boarding pass for my hop and commented that he had never seen such a lowly ranking enlisted man get a V.I.P. flight. I was walking on air! The 3rd Helicopter Company really took care of its men.

One Friday afternoon in the summer of 1965, I was cleaning up the hangar with some of my buddies when a staff sergeant crew chief came over to talk with me.

"Kelley. You're from Boston, right?"

"Yes I am."

"How would you like to crew my bird up to Boston this weekend?"

"What? Are you kidding me? I'm just a PFC. How can I do that?"

The staff sergeant went on to tell me that he was from Michigan and had no interest in going up to Boston. He also already had some plans for the weekend. He told me he would get a clearance from our sergeant first class maintenance supervisor for me to take his CH-21 to Boston. I couldn't say yes fast enough. I drew a flight helmet from supply and received the crew chief's toolbox keys. I then caught the shuttle truck up to my barracks, packed a small bag with my civilian clothes, and returned to the airfield. I then prepared the bird for the special training flight north.

As my pilots did the pre-flight inspection, I stood in front of the Shawnee. *You sure are one lucky guy to be crewing a fantastic machine like this, especially as a PFC, Kelley.* For me, it was "the big time." We took off and flew northeast over the Allegheny Mountains, where we ran into bad weather. The pilots had to fly IFR conditions, and after some very tense moments avoiding small civilian aircraft in the fog, we landed at the Allentown Municipal Airport to park for the night. While the pilots went downtown to get a hotel room, I changed into my civilian clothes and hitched a ride to get something to eat and take in a movie. I did not have enough money for a hotel room, so I returned to the airport and climbed inside the helicopter to sleep. About midnight it began to get very cold, and I began to shiver. I just could not sleep. Suddenly, I heard a knock on the cargo door and went to see who it was. An old man in his 60s was standing next to the door, holding a flashlight. It was the night watchman.

"You're making an awful lot of noise in that craft, boy. What are you doing out here so late?"

"I'm the crew chief of this bird here, and I'm trying to get some sleep. It's cold, though, and I'm having a bit of trouble."

"Well why don't you come with me and get warm for a few moments?" He gestured to his guard shack, which was about 100 feet from the helicopter. Inside his cozy little shack was a coal-fired stove with a pot of hot coffee on top. He poured me a cup and we talked for a while about Allentown.

"You know, if you want to sleep still, I have a cot in the back room over there. You're more than welcome to use it."

"Oh yes, I would. Thank you very much. You are too kind."

His hospitality was much appreciated, and I got a good night's sleep on his warm and comfortable cot. The next morning, the watchman woke me up early so I could get the bird ready for flight. My pilots showed up well-rested, and as we began to check the aircraft over, a small crowd of local civilians began to gather around the bird to have a closer look. One of the pilots waved me over to him.

"Kelley, show these people the helicopter. Let them take a good look at it. They are taxpayers and they own it. It will make them feel good to see it up close."

The ones who liked it the most were the children. I picked them up and put them inside the cargo bay, where they ran up front through the rows and bounced up and down on the V.I.P. seats. Some of the parents were veterans who asked me questions about the aircraft. After a few minutes of this show and tell, my pilots told me it was time to go. I cleared everyone out and had them step back from the aircraft. We fired up the engine, warmed everything up, and were soon airborne for Boston.

We pushed on to upstate New York and landed at Stewart Air Force Base to refuel. The radial engine had a big appetite for oil and our pilots had a standing joke whenever they refueled by telling the fuel driver to "fill the oil and check the gas." From Stewart, it was an almost straight run east to Hanscom Air Force Base, just outside of Boston.

I called my father to come out to pick me up at the air base. When he saw me securing the helicopter, he was so proud of his boy. I introduced him to my pilots and showed him the Shawnee. The pilots had relatives in the area and departed to visit them. Once I tied down the rotors and locked the bird, I was off for a short visit home. This scene repeated itself almost 40 years later, when I was on a visit to the Hanscom Air Base Post Exchange which brought back some pleasant memories. A Massachusetts National Guard UH-60 Blackhawk helicopter landed at the exact spot in front of the operations building where my old CH-21 had landed in 1965. I watched the crew chief and pilots get out of the bird and secure it.

On our return trip back to Davison, we had good VFR flying weather and made it back to base in record time. The pilots set the Old Banana down in a meadow out in the countryside for a quick pit stop before the final leg of the trip to the base. They left the rotors turning with low power while they relieved themselves, and then we pulled pitch and were off, heading southbound. We arrived in time for evening dinner, and I spent that night and the next few days bragging to all my buddies about my shot at being an acting CH-21 crew chief. Unknown to me, this little mission moved me into contention for promotion to E-4 rank. I was given a good report by the pilots, and not too long after that I was told by my platoon sergeant to prepare myself for the E-4 promotion board. I remember telling him that I was not ready for promotion, having only been in the Army for 12 months, but I nervously did as I was told.

Our unit had received a large group of veteran aircraft mechanics just back from an overseas tour of South Korea. I felt my chances of promotion were "slim to none." Salvation came in the form of current events and job occupation skills (MOS), as I was good at both. I read *Time* magazine on a weekly basis in the dayroom and knew all about the Pakistan-Indian war. When the promotion board asked me questions about these subjects, I had the answers ready. Additionally, on the CH-21, I was a walking, talking maintenance manual. But when they asked me questions about how many men made up an Army division, or what the range of a 50-caliber machine gun was, I hadn't a clue. When I left my meeting with the board, I thought I was sunk. I did not hear anything from them for some time and figured that I was not qualified for promotion. I moved on with my duties and my life.

For the rest of the summer of 1965, I enjoyed hanging out with my good friends Tommy and Dave. I had brought my car down to Virginia from Massachusetts and we had fun cruising around the local cities and towns outside Fort Belvoir, mostly looking for girls. I had owned my 1951 Mercury Coupe since my junior year in high school, and it came in handy for double dating.

One Saturday afternoon, we drove out to the skating rink in Alexandria, hoping as usual to meet girls. Tommy was the only one who could skate, so he told us to sit and wait while he went out on the rink. Tommy was a tall, handsome redhead and a very likable guy. He soon met some girls and invited them over to where we were sitting. He introduced us to his new friends and within an hour, we all had a date for the next weekend. The plan was for us to show up at the Washington Monument at noon on a Sunday. That Sunday, we waited at the monument for over an hour and just when we were about to give up on them, the girls came across the open field, calling our names. They took us to the Smithsonian Museum and then we got a tour of all the large government buildings of downtown Washington, D.C. We had a great day, and within a few weeks we were all going out on regular dates.

Being stationed at Fort Belvoir was turning into a wonderful experience for us young soldiers. But the clouds of war were closing in. That summer, President Johnson made a television announcement that he was ordering the 1st Air Cavalry Division to Vietnam. We had received some new men in our company who had come up from Fort Benning because they did not have enough time left on their enlistment to go overseas with the new cavalry division. They told us about the formation of the new division there. The 11th Air Assault Division, which I had known about while at my training at Fort Rucker, was being reflagged as the new Air Cavalry Division and sent to Vietnam as part of Johnson's buildup of American forces to fight the expanding communist attacks throughout South Vietnam.

CHAPTER FIVE

Guns and Rabbits

Pete

I was only 17 when I joined the U.S. Army on October 2, 1964. I had to get my parents' permission to enlist. They did not want me to go into the service. My father wanted me to stay in high school and attend college, like my older siblings. However, since I was a young boy, I had always wanted to be a soldier. That was my dream. I guess it was my calling.

I used to collect toy soldiers and play with them for hours, reenacting battles. I would take books out of the library on military subjects like the Revolutionary War and World War II. I spent hours watching old war movies like *The Sands of Iwo Jima* and *Pork Chop Hill*. I loved anything to do with the military. When I was in my junior year at Hull High School on Boston's south shore, I came across an issue of *National Geographic Magazine* with a photo of a U.S. Marine H-34 helicopter in a South Vietnam rice paddy. Infantrymen were slogging through the water on their way to a battle. *That is so cool, flying around in a helicopter and getting into combat. I'd like to do that too!*

The most important influence on my decision to go into the Army, however, was not the books and movies. It was a local guy named Francis Donahue. Francis was a tough Irishman who had fought in Europe as a paratrooper in the famous 82nd Airborne Division. He was one of the regular customers on my paper route when I was 12 years old. My older brother and sister had handed down their paper route to me, which gave me about fifty customers. With the money I earned from my route, I would buy *Our Army at War* comic books with "Sergeant Rock of Easy Company" and follow his monthly adventures as he took on the Nazi Infantry in World War II. Sergeant Rock was my hero, until I met Francis Donahue.

Francis owned two beagle hunting dogs that he took good care of. One day, he asked me if I wanted to look after his dogs when he went away with his buddies to hunt deer up north. I took on the job, and fed and cleaned up after his prized beagles. It wasn't long before that work paid off for me, and Francis invited me to go to his gun club to try some target shooting. The club had a small indoor range made of cement cinder blocks and an old oil stove with a pipe going up through the roof. It was very crude, but that wasn't what people came there for. The club had a 50-foot firing range with targets.

Francis introduced me to some of the weapons they had at the range. He started me off with a .22 caliber bolt action Winchester rifle, shooting at targets with bullseyes the size of a half dollar. His buddies at the range were shooting rifles with scopes on them, as they were old guys and had poor vision. One of them let me use his Winchester .52 caliber rifle with a scope on it. Back then, that was the crème de la crème of hunting rifles.

After progressing through various caliber weapons on the target range over a period of weeks, Francis thought I was ready to go hunting for small game. One of his friends loaned me a .22 caliber rifle, and I went out a few times with Francis to hunt for rabbits. I was a pretty good shot, but most of all, I learned about the great outdoors, how to track, and how to be a safe hunter. Francis opened up a whole new world to me that I had never known before. I really admired him very much. It was tough at times because Francis had many shortcomings. He spent a lot of his time down at the gun club, or the VFW Club, drinking too much, and he failed to keep many promises to me or to pay me for chores I did for him. I overlooked all that, though, because he was an alcoholic and I figured that was part of the game.

While Francis did not talk about his war experiences to me much, I found out from his buddies at the gun club that he saw a lot of combat in the war as an airborne infantryman. They told me he had served as a rifleman with the 502nd Parachute Infantry Regiment, and had jumped into Sicily and Normandy on D-Day, June 6, 1944. Joe Orlando, one of the old guys at the gun club, told me that Francis had completed four combat jumps and participated in a lot of dangerous fire fights.

"I'll tell you now, that man is one tough son of a bitch. Sometimes Frank will go into a bar and pick a fight with the biggest guy there, just for fun." Joe shook his head, but whether it was in admiration or consternation, I couldn't quite tell. "Did you know he has hearing loss in one ear? He could have easily gotten a deferment from World War II service, but he managed to enlist and become a paratrooper by learning to read lips. If you were looking at him and talking, he knew what you were saying. He was determined, that's for sure."

All of this was my real reason for going into the Army. I wanted to be an airborne infantryman like Francis Donahue. I wanted to be tough like Francis.

In my high school, there were about twenty of my classmates who quit school like me to enlist in the service. As I said before, I had a difficult time trying to convince my parents and family to let me join up. I begged my parents to let me join the Army on an almost daily basis.

Whenever I talked with my mother about it, she would start to cry and defer me to my father. My dad was a company man and worked for a big milk distributor. He had worked his way up from driving a milk delivery truck, to becoming a salesman, to getting promoted as the assistant plant manager. Whenever I brought up the Army, he told me that an education was important if I ever wanted to get a good job. Even my older brother tried to talk me out of joining.

He had graduated from college, gotten married, and had a good career at the Dover Sherman Massachusetts Regional School. I visited him a lot at his home. Whenever I would talk about the Army, he always had the same response.

"Oh Peter, cut it out. You don't want to do that."

But I did. I really did. The only thing I had in my favor was that my oldest brother was in the Coast Guard. He loved military life, and I reminded my parents of that as much as possible.

None of this kept me from going into the Army though. I was determined to have my way and I eventually wore my father down. One day, he caught me by surprise as I brought the subject up, expecting a repetition of the conversations we'd been having for the past several months.

"Okay Peter, I'll sign your consent form to join the Army."

I opened my mouth to argue further, but then the meaning of what he had just said sunk in. I was going to join the Army! Man, I was flying high that day. I couldn't wait to deliver the form to my local Army recruiter.

When my big day arrived, I reported to the recruiter's office and took the battery of aptitude tests all recruits were asked to take upon joining.

"You have some pretty good scores here, kid. You should sign up for one of the Army's technical skills jobs." The recruiter tried to hand me some informational material on all the jobs that were available. I didn't even glance at them.

"No thank you. I want to be an airborne infantryman."

He looked at me like I was crazy. "Okay, if that is what you want kid, I will sign you up for Airborne Infantry advanced training."

It was what I wanted, for sure. I signed my name to all the enlistment documents and was ready to begin my adventure as a soldier in the United States Army.

On the day of my induction physical exam, a bus took me and about thirty guys to the Boston Army Base Armed Forces Induction Center on Summer Street. It was an eight-story, city-block-long concrete building, and when we went upstairs to the second floor, there were about a hundred guys waiting around in the lobby. Some were taking the draft physical, and others were taking their entry physical exam to join the Army, Navy, Marines, and Air Force. I did not see any of my classmates from Hull High School and did not know anyone there.

They soon lined us up, made us strip down to our underwear, and began to run us through the physical examination stations. They checked our weight, height, vision, heart, lungs, and feet, looking for anything in general that would disqualify us from military service. I was a little worried because as a child I had suffered from asthma. I was not able to go out and play a lot with my neighborhood friends because things like moldy leaves or dampness would set off an asthma attack and cause me to have difficulty breathing. As a result, I missed a lot of school days.

But luckily, I passed and was classified as acceptable. My dream of being a soldier was about to begin.

They took us to a large cafeteria where we were given meatloaf, mashed potatoes, vegetables, and cold milk for lunch. It was a pretty good meal, much better than what they fed us at high school. They had us stay in the game room next to the lobby to await our induction oath. After a while, an officer called us together into a large group and began to have us repeat his words as he read the oath of enlistment. We held our right hand up as in a boy scout pledge; I tried to remember what the officer was saying but ended up just mumbling the words. There were so many of us, I figured he would never notice me. All I heard was "blah, blah, blah…" as I thought about my future as an airborne infantryman!

Finally, he finished and told us we were now in the military service. After that, they loaded us on a chartered bus and we rode down to Fort Dix, New Jersey to begin our basic training. I don't remember much about that trip. All I remember is the smell of the diesel exhaust and the humming of the wheels. I was so excited and nervous at the same time, wondering what lay ahead.

I was not a very outgoing person and did not engage in any small talk with the others on the bus. I sat in the back, lost in my thoughts, wondering if I had made the right decision to join the Army. Other than a few trips up to Maine with my parents to visit my brother at the Coast Guard base where his ship, the *Cutter Campbell*, was docked, I had never been away from my hometown before, not even to any summer camps. I did not know much of life, as I had been very protected by my family. Even in school, I was quiet and independent.

I soon discovered that the Army would change all of that, and it started with the shock this quiet, soft teenager received upon arrival at the Army Reception Center. As soon as the bus arrived on the base, my trip to Fort Dix became a visit to the worst "hell hole" I had ever known. It was too late to change my mind. I was now in the Army and about to become a soldier.

CHAPTER SIX

Airborne Infantry

Pete

The reception station was a rude awakening for me. We were told by the grizzly sergeants that we would spend a few days there getting processed into the Army before being sent to a basic training battalion. My time at the station was the beginning of some of my Army problems. I did not know anyone and felt isolated. I began to seriously question my childhood plans of being a soldier.

Every time you did not do something fast enough, the sergeants would make you drop to the ground and attempt to perform 20 push-ups as punishment. We did a lot of push-ups that first day. A sergeant formed us up and led us to an old wooden barracks, where he assigned us to a bunk bed. He then ordered us to clean up the barracks, starting with the latrine. We found some buckets, soap, brooms, and mops, and began to scrub the old World War II building.

That first night in the barracks, I did not sleep well. I was anxious about what would happen the next day. At 0400 hours, a sergeant flipped on the lights and began banging on a metal trash barrel cover to wake us up.

"Get up, get your ass out of the sack! Get moving!"

I opened my tired eyes, feeling as if I was in some kind of a cruel dream. *What is this shit? At home, I got up at 7 am for school.* After we made our bunks and cleaned up the latrine, we filed outside in the dark cold morning and got into a formation of about a hundred recruits.

By 0600 hours, we had eaten breakfast and were marched over to a large wooden building where they had a line of barbers shave off our hair. Then we went to a supply warehouse, where we were measured and issued three sets of Army fatigues and a duffle bag full of underwear, socks, shoes, and combat boots. They made us fold up our civilian clothes and pack them in our civilian travel bags. Then they mailed them to our homes. No one could have civilian clothes as they did not want anyone going "AWOL" (absent without leave). Once we were dressed in our new Army fatigues, we were lined up outside to await the sergeant's orders. I remember looking around at everyone thinking we all looked like a bunch of bald turkeys.

We soon learned that a haircut was mandatory every week for the entire eight weeks of basic training. If you failed to get your haircut, you would be put in a world of hurt by the drill sergeants.

You never knew when a sergeant would drop in and start barking orders. It seemed as though every few hours we had to stop our work and fall outside in the street for a roll call formation. The only highlights were the marches to and from the mess hall for hot meals. The chow was good, but they only gave us seven minutes to eat before they forced us out of the mess hall and back into another formation. No one was allowed to talk during the meals. You ate quickly and got outside.

During any idle time, the sergeants would make us fall out in the street and put us through "Close Order Drill," which was a review of the basic movements of all soldiers in training. We learned how to come to attention, stand at ease, stand at parade rest, line up in squad and platoon formations, march in cadence, and run at a fast pace while maintaining our formation. All of this was part of their training plan to make us work as a team and not as individuals.

Daytimes had us on stupid "make work" details, like pushing a lawn mower, police call to pick up trash, carrying garbage from the mess hall to a huge steel dumpster, or painting rocks with white paint along pathways and sidewalks.

On our third day at the reception center, the sergeants gave us the first good news we had in the three days of hell that we had so far. They called out our names and assigned us to a basic training unit. We were told to gather our gear and line up in the street to wait for an Army truck that would take us to our new BCT (basic combat training) unit. Within an hour, we were loaded onto cargo trucks and on our way to Alpha Company, 3rd Training Brigade.

We arrived at a row of old, wooden World War II barracks that were located right next to McGuire Air Force Base. A cadre of NCOs greeted us as we got off the trucks. It was mass confusion as they yelled at us to unload quickly. We struggled to carry our heavy duffle bags and jump to the ground. When I jumped off the truck, I fell down with my bag. A sergeant came over to me and kicked me in the ass.

"Get up and get your ass moving, you asshole!"

Unlike today's Army, back then, an NCO could kick you, slap you, and deal out corporal punishment as part of discipline. You dared not say anything to piss him off. The drill instructor was King Kong.

The NCOs were all in top physical condition and their uniforms were perfect. They looked like the soldier on the recruiting posters. They had us fall into a formation on the company street for a roll call. The first sergeant came out of the orderly room to give us a welcome speech and told us how in eight weeks, his NCOs would turn us into real soldiers, and that we would learn how to think and act as a team. Then he turned over the formation to his cadre of hard ass NCOs.

My platoon sergeant was an old, World War II combat veteran. Sergeant Kwader was a short, very tough Polish-American who had been a rifleman with the famous 1st Infantry Division (The Big Red One). He was the first NCO I ever saw that wore a Combat Infantry Badge on his uniform. Man, I liked the looks of that CIB and decided I was going to somehow get me one.

We soon discovered Sergeant Kwader could be a very nasty son of a bitch if you crossed him. Later, we realized that he had to be tough on us in order to make us into disciplined and competent soldiers who could follow orders under pressure. I was now part of a 40-man platoon, with four squads of ten recruits each. From that moment on, we would have to function as a team, all pulling in the same direction. Our civilian freedoms were put on hold.

The Army kept us very busy. Our days always began with Sergeant Kwader waking us up at 0400 hours and telling us to get dressed and fall out on the company street for a three-mile run. Back then, we ran with our combat boots on, not running shoes like they have now. After the first mile, the boots felt like two sidewalk bricks on your feet. By the end of the run, your lungs felt like they would burst. It's a miracle no one had a heart attack.

Some guys had a difficult time running and would fall out of formation to the side of the road, out of breath. Sergeant Kwader would yell at them to get back to the platoon and keep moving. Some guys would vomit all over themselves. Kwader would call them soft-ass civilians.

"Suck it up, recruit, and move it out!"

We thought he was a mean bastard, but by the end of boot camp, we realized he was just doing his best to turn us into soldiers. And we were very soft civilians. Hell, at home, I never even had to make my bed. My mom did that for me. Now, I not only had to make my bed, but it had to be done "Army style" with the sheets and blankets drawn tight enough to bounce a quarter coin on it, and with not even one tiny wrinkle.

Once in line, we had to stand at parade rest and study the Army's general orders which were posted on wooden signs nailed onto the mess hall building. Those orders had to be memorized. You could be called on by the sergeant or any other authority at any time, and when you were, you had to give the general orders. The order I still remember was for walking guard duty:

"Recruit! General orders!"

"To walk my post in a military manner, keeping always on alert and observing everything that takes place within sight or hearing, sergeant!"

There were several other duties we would be required to perform. There was police call, mowing grass at company or battalion headquarters, and "ash and trash," which involved going out on the back of a truck with a couple of heavy steel barrels and going around the Army post picking up litter. Most of our time, however, was in daily training.

After breakfast, we formed up our whole recruit company and marched off to a training area where we would participate in physical training (PT), hand to hand combat, bayonet drills, first aid, rifle drills, and target range, to name a few. Towards the last few weeks of basic training, we got into the core of preparing to be a soldier. This included firing our weapons, learning how to throw a live hand grenade, and going through the obstacle course, which involved crawling under barbed wire and past explosive bomb simulators while a machine gun fired two feet above your head until you reached a deep trench at the end of the course. Sometimes this training was done under difficult weather conditions, such as in the rain, crawling through mud, during a snowstorm, or in hot, humid weather with a temperature of 90 degrees and various insects crawling down your sweaty back. And always with the sergeants yelling orders and correcting any mistakes you made. Sometimes with a kick up your ass.

During all this training, I sort of kept to myself and didn't make too many friends. I guess you could say I was a "lone wolf." I followed orders and did what I was told to do, but I kept a low profile. There were a few guys I did talk with on occasion. One guy I remember was a Black kid from New York City named Jones. He was a real cool dude with a great sense of humor, not your typical tough city kid. I remember he wore eyeglasses. During my early life, I had never met any Black people, so this was a new experience for me. There were no Black kids in my high school at Hull, Massachusetts. Mostly Irish and Italian, with some Jewish kids. But I didn't have any problems with Black people. My family had raised me not to judge people by the color of their skin, so I had an open mind on race relations. Unfortunately, not everyone felt that way, which caused many misunderstandings and conflict.

My eight weeks of basic training went by fast. The long, grueling days of marching, running, field training, and rifle range training, which was my favorite, were over. My best friend all through basic was my M-14. We did almost everything together. I enjoyed firing it so much that I had managed to qualify for an Expert Rifleman Badge. In our final week, I had to turn it in and was sad to see it return to the arms room rack to await the next cycle of trainees. However, I knew I would get another rifle at Advanced Infantry Training. Basic training had given me a taste of what it was going to be like when I finally got to infantry school.

Upon completion of boot camp, the Army posted orders outside the orderly room that told us where and when we would continue with our advanced individual training (AIT) schools, where soldiers would be provided with specialty training. Some guys were headed to communications school, artillery school, electronics school, or armor school. I had enlisted for infantry school, so my orders had me posted to the advanced infantry school at Fort Dix, New Jersey.

A bus took me and a few others to the infantry school on post, where it was a different world than at basic. We were housed in a modern, three-story, red-brick dormitory building with two men to a room and lots of privacy. It was a pleasant change from the wide-open bays we had lived in for eight weeks. Not only was the living accommodation much better, but the manic tempo of basic was reduced and our training sergeants did not yell at us as much. Plus, we got more time off to go to movies, the post exchange, or the Enlisted Men's Club to drink huge pitchers of 3.2 beer and eat hamburgers. It was much less stressful. Army life was getting better every day.

The first week of infantry training, we were issued new TA-50 Field equipment and an M-14 Rifle. I had another new best friend. The bulk of our training consisted of qualifying on various types of infantry weapons, from the M-1911A1 .45 caliber automatic pistol, the M-60 7.62mm machine gun, the M-2 60mm mortar, the M-2 .50 caliber heavy machine gun, the M-18 Claymore mines, and the M-40 105mm recoilless rifle, to name a few. I loved all of them and was like a kid in a candy shop.

As is said, the Army was getting better day by day. Being paid to fire down range at targets was just fantastic to me. It was the best job in the Army. Besides getting to enjoy all those weapons, we did a lot of simulated battlefield training. We went out in the woods on patrols, attacked enemy fortifications, practiced land navigation exercises and movement to contact, using radios like the PRC-10 to communicate with a supporting infantry platoon or to request a fire support mission using mortars or artillery, and went on reconnaissance missions. The best jobs of all, for me, were the infantry assaults into enemy aggressor target zones. It was all hard and dirty work, but I loved it. Firing my M-14 almost every day was a blast. And all of it was giving me valuable experience that I could build on later in my Army service.

It wasn't all roses, though. I remember learning to disassemble, clean, and assemble a machine gun in a very cold warehouse classroom when the outside temperature was 20 degrees. Man, my fingers were frozen, but I managed to get that gun up and ready for action. Learning how to be a good infantry soldier was very important to me. I wanted to be as good as my old friend Francis.

Towards the end of my infantry training, I got a few opportunities to go home on a weekend pass to visit my family and friends. One time I went to the local VFW post to look up Francis. He was always glad to see me and was proud of my status as an infantry soldier.

Upon completion of infantry school, I was awarded the Military Occupation Specialty (MOS) of 11 Bravo 10 (11 B 10). I was as proud as a peacock because this meant I had achieved the coveted title of rifleman. I was on cloud nine and ready for action. Now it was time to put some frosting on my cake, as my next stop was airborne school.

I was glad to board the chartered bus for Fort Benning, Georgia, and leave the brutal cold weather of Fort Dix behind me. All I could think about was what it would be like to start airborne school and get my jump wings, like my hero Francis did in World War II. Some of my sergeants had warned me how difficult paratroop training was, but I was focused on one thing—getting those jump wings. I knew I could do it.

After a long road trip down south with stops at a bunch of greasy spoons on Route One, the bus arrived at Fort Benning. As soon as the bus driver opened the front door of the bus, two big sergeants got on and began yelling at us.

"Un-ass this bus now!"

There were about twenty of us on the bus, and we grabbed our duffle bags and scrambled off it as fast as we could, lining up in formation in front of the NCOs. They were a tough looking bunch, dressed in highly starched green fatigues with airborne wings over their left pockets and big, silver jump wings on their black baseball caps. We quickly found out what was in store for us during the next three weeks of airborne school. As soon as we were in formation, the NCOs dropped us down for 25 push-ups and then ran us over double time to the in-processing building to have our names and orders logged into the school's training rosters.

As we waited outside for our turn to enter the building, I looked around at my new base and noticed the three parachute training towers located on what I would later find out was called Eubanks Field. The towers were painted red and white, and they were so tall. I would soon discover that one of the towers was 34-foot tall, while the other two were 250-foot tall. It was scary to look at them. *I'm going to have to drop off those towers in a parachute.* I tried not to let my nervousness show as I looked over the rest of the base.

Many of the buildings were decorated with the large emblems of Army airborne units like the 82nd Airborne, the 101st Airborne, and the 173rd Airborne, as well as those of the various airborne regiments like the 501st, the 506th, and the 1st Special Forces Group. I noticed that a few of our sergeants wore Ranger tabs on their baseball caps. Airborne Rangers were considered to be the elite of paratroopers. *Wouldn't it be cool if I could become an Airborne Ranger?* My nervousness was temporarily overcome by excitement.

I would have to make it through jump school first. Once we were all processed in, one of the sergeants took us over to a row of old, wooden World War II barracks and told us to find a bunk and get settled in. We spent the rest of the first day cleaning the barracks and storing our gear. Then we had to complete one last formation before we got to eat chow in the airborne mess hall. Compared to infantry training, the food was very good. We quickly discovered there was good reason for this, as we would be burning thousands of calories over the next three weeks.

These three weeks would consist of three different phases of training. The first week was called ground school and consisted of a lot of running and physical fitness exercises, learning how to wear and handle a parachute, and training on parachute landing falls (PLFs). You had to land a certain way or you could get injured. The second week was tower school, where they placed you in a parachute rig and had you descend off the 34-foot tower in a simulated airborne jump. Once you mastered that, they sent you up on the 250-foot tower to do the same thing again.

Man, I was scared shitless. I had never been up that high before, not even on the Ferris wheel at Nantasket Beach. Going off that tower was very scary, especially with the jumpmaster NCOs yelling "GO-GO!" in your ears. We also learned how to form a "stick," where a group of jumpers would exit the airplane in one movement. They had "dummy"

Air Force transport aircraft on the training field that we could jump out of to simulate jumping out of a real, moving aircraft. They also made us take the Army Physical Fitness Exam that week to see if we met the fitness requirements of airborne training. I was in good shape and easily passed the test.

The third week of training was called jump week. This was when all our training paid off, as we were fitted up with a parachute and taken out to Lawson Army Airfield to board an Air Force C-130 transport plane for our first official jump. We had been trained to do a mass exit where our stick would jump together.

The plane took off and I could tell by the looks on everyone's faces that we were all nervous, not knowing what to expect. I worried about freezing in the door when my time to jump came. My stomach felt like it was full of butterflies, and I kept checking my equipment over and over. One of the guys was smart and brought some gum. He gave me a stick and I chewed on it like a dog. It seemed to help a little and I was grateful.

The plane would climb to an altitude of 1,200 feet at 150 miles per hour and follow a flight path towards the drop zone (DZ). The DZ was named Fryar Field after a World War II paratrooper who had been awarded the Medal of Honor. They chalked B-44 on my steel helmet to identify me in the jump roster as number 44 in Group B. A few minutes before the jump, the jumpmaster started yelling.

"Stand up and hook up!"

It was time.

We had to hook our static line to a wire on the roof of the plane which would open our chutes once we stepped out of the aircraft. Each man checked the chute of the man in front of him. Then, the plane arrived over the DZ and a green light came on inside the cabin.

"GO-GO-GO!"

One by one, right behind each other, our stick went out the door and into the air. As the wind buffeted us and we fell downward, the static line opened our chutes. I felt a sudden jerk as the chute opened and filled with air above my head.

"Whoooo!" I screamed, despite myself.

I cannot begin to describe the feeling of exhilaration I experienced as I glided down towards the DZ. It was the most awesome experience of my life. The only thing I consider to have come close to it was something I hadn't experienced yet but would later; being in a firefight with hot lead snapping all around you. The ground came up fast and I hit it like a rock. What a shock! I wasn't fully expecting to land so hard that first time. I did my PLF, rolled over, and got up to gather in my chute before it dragged me away. Once we had our chutes in our arms, we ran over to the side of the DZ where an Army bus waited to pick us up and return us to Lawson Airfield.

We were required to perform five jumps that week, four during daylight and one night jump. There were two things we worried about. "Streamers," which was when your chute failed to open and you dropped straight down, and the night-time jump. Both thoughts were extremely scary. We were told that on a night jump, you sometimes could not see the ground until you hit it. The jumpmasters also warned us that at night, with good moonlight, a road could look like a river.

We had a special release for landing in water that you pulled on about 20-feet above the water. It allowed you to drop free of your chute into the water, so the chute wouldn't cause you to drown. However, if you got fooled and mistook a road with a river, you would drop down and smack the pavement, which could severely injure you or kill you. Another big danger was falling into trees.

On our plane during my night jump, a hydraulic line broke and sprayed about ten guys with hot fluid which burned them. The crew chief repaired the leak, but we ended up having to jump out past the DZ. It was a very weird feeling, jumping into the dark night sky and floating down into the unknown, and it was made even stranger because the accident had caused unexpected chaos. We landed in trees and water, which you could see in the daytime so you could steer your chute away with the risers, but at night you just had to hope you landed right and didn't get injured. I got lucky and did not get injured in that jump. Not so much as a scratch on me.

I had done it! I completed all five jumps. I was as happy as a pig in mud. On the bus back to the base, I celebrated with B-43, the guy who was next to me in my stick. I didn't make many friends during training, but B-43 was a funny guy and I liked him. He was a former college student, about 22 years old, a little older than me. He was always smiling and joking around. He had been drafted and volunteered for airborne school. He told me that the Army wanted him to attend officers' training school (OCS), but he was not interested. He just wanted to become a paratrooper, like me.

I discovered later that I could have applied for OCS, as my general test (GT) aptitude score was 135; you only needed a score of 110 to go to OCS. In reality, though, I would not have made a good officer. I was a lone wolf, far too independent and outspoken. Sometimes officers must play politics, and that was not for me. I was a straight shooter who wouldn't kiss anyone's butt. I always said what was on my mind, for good or bad, which pissed some people off, but, hey, that was who I was.

Some NCOs and officers thought I was just a wise guy with a smart mouth. A punk city kid from Boston. That was the reason I never got many promotions in my early years of military service. I didn't take shit from anyone. I was a good soldier and followed orders, but I was a free thinker. That's why I liked Mike so much when we met later in Vietnam. He was a lot like me, and we were both Boston guys. We came from the same mold. Birds of a feather stick together, and so we did. From Vietnam to now. The gunner and the grunt.

At the end of jump week, we were formed up and presented with our coveted jump wings by the commanding officer. I became a full-fledged paratrooper, just like my hero Francis. He would have been so proud to see me getting my wings pinned on. The army awarded me with a new MOS, 11 B 10 P. The "P" denoted my status as a paratrooper. It meant they would pay me an extra $50 a month if I was on jump pay status.

The third stage of my Army training was now complete. Basic training, advanced infantry training, and airborne school. Completing training was a goal that I had met, and now I would go on to be assigned to my first permanent duty position with an airborne infantry unit. I had requested to be assigned to the 82nd Airborne Division, the famous unit that Francis had served in during World War II. However, the Army decided that I was needed in another famous unit, the 101st Airborne

Division. In April 1965 I packed my gear and shipped out to Fort Campbell, Kentucky, where I was assigned to the 1st Battalion, 501st Parachute Infantry Regiment, nicknamed "Geronimo." The regiment had a glorious history from World War II, and I was happy to be a paratrooper in the 501st.

In Kentucky, we did a lot of infantry patrols, field training exercises, movement to contact, and some jumps onto different DZs on post. Those jumps gave me that extra $50 a month in my paycheck, which really came in handy. A private's pay back in 1965 was only about $90 a month. The extra $50 a month made it so I was bringing in pretty good money for a 17-year-old kid whose only previous income was from a newspaper route in the old neighborhood. To give you an idea, back then a pack of smokes cost 19 cents and the movies cost 25 cents.

I used my money to fly home on weekends on the Eastern Airlines shuttle to Boston when I could. It also came in handy on my off-duty hours, when I'd go to the Enlisted Men's Club for a pitcher of 3.2 beer, or go to the bowling alley to shoot a few strings and eat a cheeseburger and fries at the snack bar for 50 cents. I also enjoyed playing the pinball machines and pool games in the unit's dayroom with the guys. We could also watch TV after evening meals up until 2300 hours in the dayroom. Life was good. I was in top physical condition. I was an airborne infantryman and had achieved my boyhood dreams.

The only thing missing was a real war which I could apply my new skills to. I had been watching the news on the TV every night and knew that President Johnson was ramping up deployments of troops to the war zone. I wanted to be a part of that action. A real shooting war.

The Marines had landed at Da Nang, and the Army's new 11th Air Mobile Division was reflagged to the 1st Air Cavalry Division and was on its way to the war. I went down to the administrative office and filled out a DA Form 1049 for transfer to the war zone, but the 101st would not release me from duty.

During the summer of 1965, my unit won the top honors as the best battalion in the division. Our reward was to deploy up to West Point and provide infantry weapons training to the cadets. It was a fantastic duty, and the best part was I got to go home on weekends, as West

Point was close to Massachusetts. One of our sergeants owned a car (POV—privately owned vehicle) and gave me rides to Route 28 outside Boston. One time, he failed to pick me up and I was forced to take a bus to New York City where I could transfer to the bus to West Point. Unfortunately, upon arrival at the transit terminal in New York City, I realized I was out of money and could not afford a ticket.

I saw a few Army military policemen on duty and asked them for help. The bastards took me to Fort Jay and put me in jail, where I was forced to spend the night with a bunch of drunks and petty criminals. The next day, I was released and got lucky. I ran into an Army airborne sergeant major and told him what happened to me. He saw my airborne wings with the 501st red tab and took me to the post finance office, where they gave me a travel voucher to pay for my bus fare to West Point. That was the day I discovered paratroopers take care of their own.

Back at Fort Campbell, after our tour was over at West Point, I kept thinking about Vietnam. I went to see the on-post Army recruiter to find out if he could help me get there. I was determined to go. The sergeant told me that if I took a short discharge and re-enlisted, I could get an assignment to the 1st Air Cavalry Division. That sounded good to me.

I signed the paperwork and was discharged for one day. When I returned the next day, I was sworn in and got my orders for the 1st Air Cavalry in Vietnam. I went home on a 30-day leave to say goodbye to my family and friends. My parents begged me not to go, but I was my own man and was eager for duty in Vietnam. I was now 18, an adult, and responsible for my actions. This was my master plan, and I was focused on being a combat soldier, just like Francis. I was now an airborne infantryman and my duty was to go to war. No one could change my mind.

When my leave was over, I caught a jet plane out of Boston and arrived at the Oakland Army Base, where I processed in and was placed on an overseas deployment roster. I spent a few days there waiting to ship out. There were thousands of troops processing through, arriving back from or shipping out to Vietnam and South Korea. It was a huge "repo depot." Soon, I boarded a chartered jet airliner with about a hundred other soldiers and we flew out of San Francisco Airport to Hawaii, and then onto Guam.

It was a very long flight over the vast Pacific Ocean. We arrived in Saigon at Tan Son Nhut Air Base, and I had to stay over at an Army replacement depot (Camp Alpha) for a few days until they processed me for transport up country to An Khe, the home base of the 1st Air Cavalry Division. It was hot and humid, and the place smelled funny. Not a nice smell, I'll tell you.

Upon arrival at An Khe, I was sent to the division's replacement depot (a different one) to be processed for assignment to a unit. I had assumed I would be sent to one of the big infantry brigades as a rifleman, so I was surprised when I was sent to the 1st Squadron, 9th Cavalry, a reconnaissance unit that provided the division with intelligence on enemy movements and positions out in the jungle. I didn't mind, though. All I needed was a rifle, plenty of ammunition, and some targets to shoot at. The 1st of the 9th Cavalry gave me all three.

CHAPTER SEVEN

Going to War

Mike

November 1965. I passed the E-4 board with flying colors! That meant more pay and admission to the NCO Club on post. It was the big time for me, going from a private to a specialist four. This was equal to being a corporal. The board had granted me a waiver for my time in service. I was told that there weren't too many PFCs with only 14 months in the Army who made it to pay grade E-4. But, thanks to an outstanding recommendation from my platoon sergeant, I had made the cut.

Then there was some bad news. A large levy came down from the Pentagon requesting more troops for South Vietnam. As I was walking out of the mess hall on a Friday evening, the company clerk called me over.

"Kelley. Your request for Thanksgiving leave has been granted. You have a 19-day leave en route."

"What do you mean I have a 19-day leave en route? I only asked for a five-day leave!"

The company clerk looked at me with sad eyes. "I'm sorry, Kelley, but you are on a levy to Vietnam. You've got 19 days' leave before you ship out!"

I was in shock. I felt like I had been just handed a death sentence. Back at my barracks, I went to see an older soldier who had done a tour of duty in Vietnam in 1964.

"I just found out I'm shipping out. You were there recently, what's it really like? What's going to happen?"

"Don't sweat it, kid. You're a mechanic. They'll probably have you assigned to some rear area maintenance base far from the action. It'll be okay, you'll see."

His words of reassurance did not help me. I felt doomed. On Monday morning, I reported to the orderly room to pick up my orders. I held them in my hands and slowly read each word on the official paper. I read them over and over, in disbelief that this was happening to me. It seemed like a bad dream.

SPECIAL ORDERS: Number 214

8 NOVEMBER 65

TC 243—Following reassignment directed.

KELLEY, Michael L. SP4 HHC, Davison U.S. Army Airfield, Fort Belvoir, Va.

Assigned to: 1st Cavalry Division APO, San Francisco 96307

Temp address: 134 5th Street, Cambridge, Mass.

Leave data: 19 Days approved leave en route

BPED: 17 Aug 64

ETS: 16 Aug 67

EDCSA: 1 Dec 65

Auth: DA Ltr EPADR-E-P Subj: Enl Pers Sel for OS (SEPOS)

Pacific, dtd 26 Oct 65

Special instructions: WP OA: 12 Nov 65. Presb alw of cloth and equip WB hand carried to USAREPLSTA. Indiv will have in his poss final Post clnc & compl 201 file to incl FDRF. Prov AR 612-35 (POR) apply. EM will arrive in Vietnam wearing khaki trousers & a short sleeve shirt and will have basic work uniforms and combat boots. Plague immunizations are required.

OFFICIAL WILLIAM L. CAUBUTT

1st Lt. AGC

Adjutant

My last few days with the company were spent asking a lot of questions from veteran pilots and sergeants who had been to Vietnam. No one seemed to be particularly worried.

"Kelley, I was with the cav back in '51, and it was a dam' good outfit, son. You'll be okay. Just do what the NCOs tell you to do." An old staff sergeant who served with the 1st Cavalry in the Korean War shook my hand and gave me a pat on the back. "Good luck, kid!"

Good luck. I would need a lot more than good luck going to a war zone. The prospect of getting shot at like my pilots didn't make the situation any better.

Just before I left, all my buddies got together to give me a nice sendoff party. They all told their best jokes to cheer me up. I put my best face forward and tried not to show how scared I was. I was just a kid who, until recently, had barely been out of Boston, and now I was going to Vietnam. I was going to war.

On the trip home to see my family and friends, I wondered how they would take the news. I was afraid of upsetting my mother, for she had been against my joining the Army in the first place. I sat in my bedroom at home and thought about how, just a year before, I had been a teenager enjoying life with my neighborhood friends, without a care in the world. And now, I was going off to a fate unknown.

The last few days on leave were a blur, as I went around seeing all my relatives and friends before I left. I gave my father the keys to my car and asked him to look after it for me. My brother George took me to Logan International Airport in Boston to see me off. We were joined by his wife, Jo Ann, and my Aunt Loretta. My parents could not bear to see me board the plane, so they stayed home. I walked up the stair ramp to the sleek American Airlines 707 jetliner and took a seat up front, next to a window. It was a late November day, and the sky was overcast with a light drizzle. Small droplets of rain ran down the window glass as I took my final glance at my family standing at the departure gate. *This is the last time I will ever see them. I'm going to Vietnam and won't come back alive!*

The plane took off and I settled in for the long flight to San Francisco. Next to me sat a mother and her pretty, teenage daughter. We chatted some and they asked me where I was from and how I liked Army life. As we talked, the stewardess came by and passed out some magazines. She handed me a copy of *Time* magazine, and on the cover was a bleak photograph of wounded soldiers in a battle at a place called the Michelin Rubber Plantation in South Vietnam.

"Pardon me ladies, but I would like to read this if you don't mind."

I turned the pages to read the story of the battle. As I got deeper into the magazine, another story caught my eye. The 1st Cavalry Division had engaged in battle in the Ia Drang Valley with a large North Vietnamese unit. Casualties were heavy. There were black and white photos of some of the wounded. My face turned ashen, and I began to sweat.

"Are you ok?" I looked up to see the young girl in the seat beside me looking concerned. "Are you getting air sick?"

"Yes." I didn't want to let on the real reason for my diminished pallor. "Please, excuse me for a moment."

I went to the lavatory to try and regain my composure. I looked into the small mirror and saw a very scared boy looking back at me. I splashed some cold water on my face and returned to my seat, trying to act like everything was okay. If anyone noticed my trembling hands, they made no mention of it.

When the 707 landed in San Francisco, I met up with a fellow soldier from Boston who was also going to Vietnam. We took a bus over to the big Oakland Army Base and reported in for processing. The base was jam packed with soldiers. Some were shipping out, while others were on their way home. This would be my temporary home for the week before I was ready for overseas shipment.

The base was a lot different to a regular Army post. It was basically a very long warehouse, about the length of three city blocks, compared to the separate wooden or brick barracks found on Army posts. It was equipped with everything needed to process troops. There were about four or five levels of floors above the main drag, with open bays lined with endless metal bunk beds. Below, there was a huge, consolidated mess hall, a large recreation room, a barbershop, a tailor shop, and a post exchange. At the end of the main street was a snack bar, a beer hall, and a Service Club. It was, in itself, a small city.

The beer hall was always crowded and noisy, as were the barracks bays. One night, there was a group of returning combat veterans from the 101st Airborne Brigade holding court near my bunk. The paratroopers were a happy, rowdy bunch, full of bravado and beer. They told war stories to anyone who would listen. As they talked, more and more new guys gathered around the group and sat on the floor to listen and watch. It was theater as fine as you would find in any cultured community.

One veteran, the best talker, provided narration, and the others backed him up with words, sound effects, and gestures. They described battles, ambushes, and firefights, talked about killing the Viet Cong and North Vietnamese, getting shot at and wounded, and getting lost in the jungle. They had us on the edge of our seats as they described what it felt like to be almost overrun by their fierce enemy.

Their description of what it was like flying in an assault helicopter grabbed my interest. I saw them hanging out the open doors with their boots on the skids, firing their weapons into the jungle as the helicopter flared into a hot landing zone under enemy machine-gun fire. I was terrified, but I couldn't stop myself from listening.

These veterans were not much older than me, maybe 21 or so, yet they had a hardened, worn look about them, with eyes that darted about the room like a tiger's. They kept us up until the lights went out, and left us new guys with more thoughts than some of us wanted on what lay in store for us when we got to the war zone. That night, sleep did not come easy. My mind was full of wild stories of men killing and getting killed. Visions of green jungles and helicopters kept running through my head. None of the tales my former pilots or sergeants told me were anything like the nightmarish stories the young paratroopers had just told. I did not know it at the time, but there was a good reason for this difference in the war stories. The war had changed a lot between the battles of 1963 and the large-scale unit battles of 1965. The insurgent war had been fought by small bands of Viet Cong, who were being replaced by the North Vietnamese infantry battalions infiltrating down the Ho Chi Minh Trail into South Vietnam. By November 1965, it was a whole new war. And Uncle Sam had invited me to his *new* war game. It was called "Search and Destroy."

When I arrived at the 1st Cavalry base camp at An Khe in early December 1965, the clouds were hanging low and a misty rain covered the surrounding mountains. The Air Force C-130 cargo plane that dropped us off kept its engines running at full power. As soon as we scrambled off the ramp, outgoing troops ran up it, and the big silver bird quickly taxied away before the loadmaster had closed the rear ramp door. *Those Air Force pilots must be in a hurry to get home for dinner.* I soon found out they were moving fast because the local Viet Cong enjoyed dropping mortars onto the runway.

I was in a small group of new soldiers, and we stood in a light drizzle, getting wet as we waited for a ride to the base. A beat-up looking Army 2½ ton cargo truck arrived and picked us up to take us to the repo depot. We signed in and were issued a regulation Army "pup" tent to sleep in. It rained almost all night, and everything was cold and damp. We were up in the mountains of the Central Highlands, where it was a lot cooler than the rest of tropical Vietnam. It was a scary night, filled with strange sounds and sights. All night long, artillery boomed in the distance and flares drifted in the darkness until they fizzled out near the ground. Searchlights played back and forth across nearby Hon Cong Mountain. I looked forward to the morning, when I would join my new unit.

When dawn finally arrived, I was given a cup of Army coffee, known as "lifer brew," and some lukewarm scrambled eggs. We waited around to begin the paperwork for our assignment to one of the division's units. The sergeants broke us up into small groups and lined us up outside a large, general-purpose tent (GP tent). I saw helicopters flying overhead. *Surely, I'm going to one of those units to join a maintenance crew.* The 1st Cavalry had over 400 helicopters, and as a mechanic, it would be only natural that I should be placed in a maintenance support unit.

It was just a matter of putting me where I was needed. The 15th Maintenance Battalion was the main helicopter repair unit at An Khe, located on a huge, sprawling heliport called the Golf Course. I assumed I would be sent there. The 15th Battalion was responsible for all the major work on Army aircraft. I had to be going to the 15th.

When my orders were finally processed, they said I was going to a unit called the 1st Squadron, 9th Cavalry. I had no idea what kind of unit it was, but I thought for sure it was some kind of maintenance unit. A sergeant came out of the tent and ordered us to load up into the back of a cargo truck for a ride to our new units. About twenty guys were on the back of the truck as it wound its way up a muddy road towards the center of the base camp.

When we reached the top of a hill, we could see the whole valley, including the Golf Course. It was about a mile wide and filled with hundreds of helicopters as far as you could see, from twin rotor CH-47 Chinooks to small OH-13 aircraft. Most of the aircraft we saw were UH-1 Hueys. It seemed as though every helicopter the Army owned was parked on the Golf Course. The sight of them all was breathtaking. Rows and rows of aircraft lined up in tactical formations, some on special metal helipads called PSPs.

Above us, barely visible in the gray, overcast sky, were helicopters buzzing back and forth on missions. In the near distance, the Hon Cong Mountain dominated the valley. Its top was shrouded in a misty fog. At the very top was an Army radio relay station.

As the truck wound its way along the twisting road, up and down small hills, we stopped at different units to let off troops. The sergeant would get out of the truck and call off the names of the men and their units.

"Jackson, Simpson, Casey, Ravello. This is it, men. Grab your bags and get off the truck. You are now at 1st Brigade!"

The troops picked up their bags and walked up a dirt road leading to their new unit. The truck then lurched to a start and continued up the road before once more coming to a stop.

Finally, we arrived at my new unit.

"Kelley, Youse!" We jumped off the truck and picked up our bags. The NCO pointed to a dirt road in front of us. "That's your new unit, men. The 1st of the 9th. Just go up the road to the headquarters and report in."

As John and I walked up the dirt road, we began to talk about what this new unit was all about. We were both helicopter mechanics. He had just come from an assignment in West Germany.

"Why did you leave?"

"I volunteered to go. I wanted to see some action."

John was a short, handsome guy with black hair from New Mexico. Today you would say he looked like Tom Cruise. And he was just as cool and gutsy as the actor was in his films.

When John and I reached the headquarters orderly room, they looked at our orders and told us to report in to Troop C (Charlie Troop). We walked a short distance across the road and entered the worn tent that was Troop C's orderly room. We were met by the first sergeant, Joe Baron, a small, wiry NCO with a stern face. He took us over to the troop commander's tent for an interview.

"Sit down men, make yourselves comfortable." The commander gestured towards some homemade chairs as we entered the tent. "I'm Major Billy Joe Nave, from Tennessee. Where are you two from?"

Major Nave was a short, stocky, and handsome blond career aviator in his early 30s. He put us at ease right away with his friendly personality.

"New Mexico."

"I come from Boston."

"What kind of training do you two have?"

"We are both helicopter mechanics, ready to fix some birds." I was a bit nervous at this point, as I hadn't seen much that looked like a place where they would be repairing helicopters near our new unit.

"Men, we are in dire need of replacements like you. We just came out of a battle in the Ia Drang Valley and need all the help we can get. We especially need a couple of good crew chiefs. I am going to assign you both to be crew chiefs on our Hueys. You will be placed on flight status immediately."

"Flight status?" *I don't want any part of flying in Vietnam.* "There must be some kind of mistake. Sir, I am a mechanic. I just work on helicopters, I can't fly in them as a crew chief. And besides, I never went to tech school for the UH-1 Huey. I'm only qualified on OH-13s and CH-21s."

Major Nave grinned. "Kelley, did that OH-13 have a large main rotor and a small tail rotor?"

"Yes sir, it did!"

"Good, so does the Huey! Now get your ass down to the flight line and report to Sergeant Guadalupe in the weapons platoon. Dismissed!"

Like it or not, John and I were now Huey crew chiefs in this new unit. We picked up our bags and received directions from the first sergeant to go down a small dirt path to a large GP tent where the weapons platoon was quartered. We each found a canvas cot and put down our bags. I looked the place over. It was an old, worn-out tent with a dirt floor and a single light bulb hanging from a center support pole. A few troops were sitting on their cots, talking and cleaning their weapons. John and I introduced ourselves.

"Where's the platoon sergeant?" John seemed to be more eager than I was to see some action.

"He's down at the flight line. It's probably best to wait for him to return."

We waited for our new leader, listening to the men talk about their helicopter missions. Almost all of them were veterans of the battle of Ia Drang Valley. By late afternoon, the tent began to fill up with more men, most of whom were either crew chiefs or door gunners in the weapons platoon, also called the gunship platoon. Once they found out we were new guys, they began to tell us stories of their missions in the Ia Drang.

It wasn't long before John and I realized that we were not in any type of maintenance unit. Nope, this was strictly a front-line combat unit. Our unit's job was to fly recon missions, scouting patrols at treetop level to search for enemy forces in the jungle. In other words, they went out looking for action every day. I was in the last place I wanted to be. Right in the middle of the shooting war at the point of the spear.

CHAPTER EIGHT

Aero Rifle Blues Platoon

Pete

An Khe base camp was a huge valley carved out of the jungle, encircled with concertina wire and a string of defense bunkers made from stacks of sandbags reinforced with PSP, a sheet of steel used for making aircraft runways that had holes punched out every few inches. It was a very sturdy material and came in handy for making a roof over the bunkers.

Inside the perimeter was the largest helicopter landing field I ever saw. Rows and rows of Army helicopters stretched out before me as far as the eye could see. *That's a good target for enemy mortar fire. Those heloes are like sitting ducks.*

In my new unit of assignment, we had about thirty helicopters. The Infantry Blues Platoon had what was called a lift platoon consisting of five UH-1D infantry transports that we termed "Slicks" because they did not have heavy armament on them like the Huey gunships. A Slick had a pair of M-60D 7.62mm machine guns mounted on each side of their open doorway. The crew chief fired one gun and a rifleman fired the other gun.

I was pumped up and eager to go out on one of the Slicks to see some action. I saw myself flying out to the jungle and jumping off the helicopter into combat. But first, I had to get processed into my new unit. I met First Sergeant Joe Barron, a short, tough-looking career soldier who took me down to the infantry tent, a large GP tent that could hold about forty men. He introduced me to a sergeant and some of the men in the rifle platoon. The platoon was called the "Blues" for the color of the infantry blue. They seemed sort of standoffish and not too friendly, but that did not bother this Lone Wolf. I did not give a shit. All I wanted was to get my hands on a rifle and some ammunition and go out hunting for some Viet Cong.

After I found an empty canvas Army cot and dropped my duffle bag, I was told to report to the supply tent to draw my equipment. The Supply NCO issued me basic TA-50 field gear consisting of a sleeping bag, air mattress, steel helmet with liner and camo cover, web gear, canteen, first aid kit, an M-7 bayonet with a scabbard, and a black plastic rifle they called the M16E1 rifle with extra magazine clips. I was trained mostly on the M-14 Rifle, but the Army made a last-minute switch to the lighter M-16 for Vietnam. It proved to be a big mistake, as we learned in combat, because it had a bad habit of jamming up during firefights.

The platoon sergeant welcomed me to his platoon and told me the mission of the 1/9th Cav Blues was to go out into the jungle on ground reconnaissance missions and look for evidence of enemy activity in areas where the division intelligence suspected infiltration. If we were successful, we would locate and engage enemy forces and try to hold them in contact until our commander was able to call in for an air assault by one of the large infantry battalions in the three brigades of the 1st Cavalry Division. Once the reinforcements arrived at our jungle location, usually in a landing zone (LZ), they would pile on, take over the fight, and our small recon platoon would be extracted and flown back to our base.

The division commander, Major General W.O. Kinnard, called the 1-9th Cav Recon "The Eyes and Ears of the Cav." If the enemy was out there, we would find him, and the division would mount a major operation to destroy him. It was a very exciting job and a bonus to be flying into battle aboard a UH-1D Huey into hot LZs.

In early December of 1965 I began going out on jungle patrols, learning from the other guys and my NCOs how to conduct myself. I liked my new platoon leader, Captain Charles "Chuck" Knowlen. He was very squared away and knew his shit. He had been involved in the famous battle of Ia Drang Valley on November 3, 1965, where he had sprung an ambush on a North Vietnamese patrol at a place called LZ Betty a few weeks before the 7th Cavalry was involved in the LZ X-Ray battle.

My squad leader was Sergeant Medina of 4th Squad. He assigned me to carry a PRC-10 radio (Prick-10). When we went out on patrols, I had to hump that radio all over the place, regardless of the heat and humidity. I did not like that duty at all. The radio man, called the "RTO," was a bullet magnet, a prime target for enemy snipers. I was never told where we were going or why. I was just a low grade, private first class "grunt." When Sergeant Medina told us to grab our gear and mount up for an air assault mission, I just followed his orders, climbed into the Huey Slick, and then once on the ground in the LZ, I looked for targets to shoot at.

When we were not out on missions, we did a lot of work projects in basecamp. Things like cutting down small trees and brush to improve the perimeter, digging foxholes and fighting positions, filling sandbags for bunkers, going out on night perimeter duty, burning shit in cut down 55-gallon drums with diesel fuel, pulling KP at the mess tent, and checking our gear and weapons.

Our living conditions were the pits. The large GP tent was dark and moldy, and the canvas cots would tear open from jungle rot. That damp mold was not good for my asthma and sometimes I had trouble sleeping in that dirty, smelly tent. The tropics were a breeding ground for millions of bacteria spores that grew on everything, from the jungle vegetation to your skin. It was dark and wet in the jungle. After a while, even the stuff I had inside my duffle bag got mold on it. Vietnam was a very humid place, and everything would get jungle rot; uniforms, boots, web gear, feet, everything. I was better off when we were out in the boondocks on a 30-day operation, when I lived in my pup tent. The air was much cleaner than in the damp, dark GP tent. I would have liked to stay, but I had to go back.

One day, down at the flight line where our Slicks were parked behind sandbag revetments, I was helping our crew chief on Slick Number 4 when I met SP4 George Gavaria, from Chicago, who was a crew chief-door gunner in the weapons platoon. He showed me how to wash my fatigues in aviation jet fuel to clean off grease and stains before rinsing them in my steel helmet with soap and water. That was a pretty good trick. George was a great guy and everyone in the troop liked him. He was always willing to help anyone.

George was a friend of Mike Kelley, another crew chief and door gunner. I arrived in Troop C before Mike, and did not hook up with him until later in my tour when we were both back at base camp in An Khe. One day, some guy asked me if I knew Kelley from Boston. Once I found out he was a Boston guy, I introduced myself and we began to hang around together. We had a lot in common, like our dislike for those "pussy" draft dodgers from Boston who burned their draft cards and evaded serving their country. Mike was Regular Army, like me, a volunteer.

Whenever possible, Mike and I would ask the first sergeant for a pass to go down into An Khe Village to get a haircut and a cold drink. We had a lot of fun together down in the ville. We didn't know it then, but after Vietnam, we would stay in touch with each other and remain good friends.

For the past 20 years, Mike has been trying to get me to talk about my experiences in the war, but I have tried to put that in my past and forget about it. Vietnam was a dark place for me to return to, but Mike kept telling me how important it was to tell our story. He kept telling me that "history untold is history lost." So, a few years ago, realizing time was going by fast and we were getting old, I called him up and told him I was ready to help him write about our experiences in Troop C, 1st Squadron, 9th Cavalry. He told me we would write our stories in our own words, not some non-veteran writer who never went through what we went through in Vietnam. We were the "Brotherhood of War," and our voices would tell the story of the Air Cavalry in Vietnam.

One day in late November, General Westmoreland showed up at the 1st of the 9th to pin medals on some of our troops for their actions in the Ia Drang campaign. He gave us a pep talk about how brave our troops were. "Westy" had his arm in a cast, and he joked how he injured it playing tennis in Saigon. I was in the front of the Blues Platoon and was only maybe eight feet from the general:

"You men have done a hell of a job in this campaign, and I am real proud of you! You guys find them and kill as many as you can, and we'll get the rest of the guys to help you out!"

Our unit, the 1st Squadron, 9th Cavalry, had one of the highest kill ratios in the division because we found the enemy first. That was our job, to find the enemy by conducting recon missions in enemy territory. From the border of Cambodia, across the Central Highlands, and over to the mountains and seacoast of the Binh Dinh province, we hunted them down. Those of us in the Blues had our own Air Force and artillery support. Our gunships in the weapons platoon were armed with rockets and machine guns, and could swoop down low and slow over a hot LZ and blast the enemy with their deadly firepower.

That is what Mike Kelley did, firing his M-60 door gun at the enemy to pin them down as we exited our helicopters. If we ran into enemy fortified bunkers, we would call in the 2nd Battalion, 20th Aerial Rocket Artillery to destroy the bunkers and kill lots of the enemy. Our gunships gave us instant suppressive fire support.

A typical air assault insertion would be an "eagle flight" of five of our UH-1D Huey Slicks. The Blues Lift Platoon flew our rifle platoon into a suspected enemy location. Above us would be our gunships buzzing overhead like angry hornets. As we came into the LZ, the pilots would flare out and stop a few feet above the ground and we would bail out and establish a secure perimeter until all the choppers had unloaded the troops into the LZ. Then our platoon leader and squad leaders would lead us forward towards our objective. The big infantry brigades would be in reserve, awaiting our contact with the enemy. If we made contact, a firefight would ensue, and we would try to hold until one of the brigades could send out an infantry company or a whole battalion to take over and box the enemy in from escape. Then it was time to call in field artillery or TAC AIR from the Air Force to drop bombs.

We used to work a lot with the 8th and 12th Cavalry Regiments. They would come out to our LZ for a big air assault aboard the UH-1D Slicks of the 227th or 229th Assault Helicopter Battalions. Then they would pile on and try to overrun the enemy positions, while gunships and Scouts would fly along the enemy's flanks to cut off anyone trying to exfiltrate the battle zone. Those battles could last anywhere from two hours to all day, depending on the strength of the enemy.

The 1st of the 9th was a special team with its own aircraft. If we had wounded or KIAs (killed in action), our own lift pilots would fly out to the LZ, and at high risk to themselves, while under enemy fire, come into the LZ whether it was day or night to evacuate our men and fly them back to the medical station. We knew our pilots had our backs. Chief Warrant Officer (CWO) Jim Reid was our lift platoon lead, and he was an expert helicopter pilot. Each of our Huey Slicks had a number on the nose from one to five. My squad, the 4th, had lift ship number four. On its nose was a painting of the head of a green python with white wings. On the side doors was a big yellow circle with the number four to identify it as a Troop C helicopter. We called it our "Air Taxi." Anytime my squad moved anywhere, it was aboard Slick number four.

We did not have to wait for anyone to pick us up. Captain Knowlen would get on the radio net and call the troop CP for an extraction. Then the lift platoon would fly out to the LZ and pick us up. No bullshit excuses, if they could take off and get through any weather, they would get us. Our pilots lived out in the boonies with us and were always on standby. We ate and slept near them, and we were like family.

We were not bogged down with cumbersome formations of battalions and command and control. We were a light Air Cavalry unit that would deploy lighting strikes by going in as a small recon unit and locking horns with the enemy. In many cases, the enemy outnumbered us, especially if we ran into a regimental headquarters. We would hold onto the contact for dear life until one of the infantry battalions could join the battle.

Some of the commanders of big infantry battalions and brigades did not admire our unit and the way we operated. However, the division commander used to say that we were the "Eyes and Ears" of the 1st Cavalry Division, and that all major battles and campaigns were based on our special skills in finding the enemy out in the vast expanse of jungle. We took a lot of pride in what he said, and knew we were a very unique unit.

Some historians have said that we were an elite unit. There is a Vietnam War movie based on our unit called Apocalypse Now, and our fearless squadron commander, Lieutenant Colonel John B. Stockton, whose character was Lieutenant Colonel Bill Kilgore (Robert Duvall). Our combat record is based on our unit's motto: "We can, we will." We killed more enemy troops than any other unit in the Vietnam War. Someday, a former North Vietnamese or Viet Cong soldier will write a book like this one about his unit and he will mention the combat effectiveness of the 1st of the 9th Cavalry.

On our recon patrols we never knew what we would encounter. If it was a small enemy unit, we would battle it out using our small arms, rifles, machine guns, and grenades. But if it was a large enemy force, we would fall back and call in our gunships to work the area over. Sometimes, we would find a small group at a river or a stream gathering water or maybe a platoon going down a trail. Other times, we would drop down right on top of them and all hell would break loose, like the time we landed on the Crow's Foot Mountain battle where elements of a regiment were dug inside fortifications and foxholes in deep elephant grass. For sure, we took our licks and got battered by the enemy on occasion, but our overall success was high.

Another kind of mission we often went on was to secure a crash sight. Sergeant Medina would order us to mount up and we would take off on our Huey Slicks and fly out to a remote area such as Dak To or the An Lao Valley and secure a helicopter that had crashed. We would set up a security perimeter around the aircraft and assist the injured crews into one of our Slicks, so they could be flown back to base. Eventually, a recovery aircraft such as a CH-54 Skycrane or CH-47 Chinook would fly out, pick up the downed bird by a sling load, and take it back to An Khe to the aircraft maintenance shop. We took off all the weapons and equipment from the aircraft before the bird was evacuated. Then our Lift Slicks would come out to extract us. Most of the time, we had no clue where we were being sent to or what the big picture was. We lived in our own little world of the platoon and squad. We were just little ants in a large army.

They called us "ground pounders" and "grunts." That was okay by me. I was proud to be a grunt. I was a combat infantryman and liked my job shooting my rifle, my best friend. When it got empty and hungry, I fed it more ammo, and I kept it cleaned, ready for action. Captain Knowlen used to tell us, when we went out on patrols, to stay tight and not get lost in the jungle. Getting separated from your squad was the worst thing to happen to a grunt. If you got lost in the bush, you were screwed. It happened to me once in Bong Son and It scared the crap out of me. I was very lucky to find my way back to my squad.

Sometimes we went through remote villages and took sniper fire. If the village was hostile, we would torch it, and burn down all the hootches, especially if we took any KIAs or wounded. That would piss us off. The locals would plead with us that their village was not a VC village, but if we found weapons or took sniper fire, our attitude was, "Fuck them!" They are all Viet Cong. Our motto was, "If it runs, shoot it."

A typical haul would be some old French MAS-36 or Japanese bolt action rifles, a few American M-1 Carbines and French MAT-49 sub-machine guns, some rice bags full of ammunition, and a few hand grenades and Soviet SKS semi-automatic rifles. I captured a French MAS-36 on one of these missions and found it to be a nice weapon. Some guys picked up a few AK-47s while on patrols.

Booby traps were something we had to be constantly aware of, as the enemy was expert at setting them out. We also had to look out for "Punji Sticks" that were usually set up next to possible landing zones. If we weren't careful, we would jump out of the helicopter and land on a bunch of them. The enemy dipped them in human waste or buffalo shit to make them toxic, and they would cause a serious infection if one cut open your leg.

It wasn't just the enemy that made life miserable for us. There were several other things to look out for in the jungle, among them the leeches and mosquitoes that would suck on your blood, or worse. When you were going across rivers or through the dense jungle, tiny, slimy leeches would enter your pants through the front flap and stick to your crotch and legs, and even enter your penis. That was damn painful, I'll tell you. The life of a grunt—humping through the jungle, sometimes up mountains under a hot sun, the rainfall, slippery, muddy trails, and always the constant thirst—it wasn't easy.

And did I mention snakes? Yeah, those green pythons were badass snakes. You did not mess with them. They were hard core NVA snakes

Pvt. Kelley arrives at helicopter tech school.

Pvt. Kelley with aviation students marching.

Pvt. Kelley at CH-21 Tech School.

Capt. Kelley, ANC, and Pvt. Kelley, Texas, November 1964.

PFC Kelley at Stewart AFB, NY with CH-21.

Tommy and Mike in a 1951 Mercury Coupe.

Going to Vietnam. Clark AFB, P.I. December 1965.

9th Air Cavalry Insignia, Vietnam.

Major Billy Joe Nave, Troop C commander.

Troop C Huey gunships over the Central Highlands.

An Khe Flight Line, UH-1B gunships, December 1965.

SP4 George L. Gavaria, Huey gunship crew chief.

Gunship pilots of 063 in flight over Bong Son.

Rocket run on enemy target in the An Lao Valley.

SP5 Walt Titchnell, expert gunship door gunner.

PFC Hosie Ward, door gunner, Gunship 063.

Major Nave's gunship shot down over Bong Son.

Remains of Major Nave's gunship at LZ Dog.

SP4 Kelley inside his UH-1B Gunship 063, Phu Cat.

CWO Frank Hiser and his UH-1B Huey Gunship.

Close up of Huey Gunship XM-16 weapons.

SP4 Kelley with his Gunship 063 "Mr. Huey."

Ia Drang battle gunship pilots at Pleiku, November 1965.

CWO Heffner and his Blues Squad at Kontum.

Troop C Blues on air assault near Cambodian border, 1966.

Alpha Troop Blues on combat mission.

Blues on security patrol outside perimeter.

PFC Burbank sights his M-60 MG at Kontum.

Captain Knowlen and RTO Smoky, Bong Son.

Blues RTO in mountains of Bong Son.

Blues going out on mission at Dak To.

Aero Scouts, Lt. Crawford and SP4 Denning at Kontum.

Blues Black, Burbank, Zimmerman, Willis, Smoky, Byrd, Koch (KIA).

SP4 Hector Aviles, Delta Troops Recon Platoon.

CWO Grimm taking on fuel with his OH-13S Chase Ship.

Troop C mess hall crew: Zim, Coshey, Cook Scotty, and unknown.

Pet mascot monkey "Hector." One of three pet monkeys; the others were called "Mandrake" and "Charlie."

SP4 Kelley at Kontum with OH–13S Scout Bird, 1966.

Ia Drang Valley recon, Lt. Crawford and SP4 Kelley.

Good shot of the Ia Drang River. Lt. Crawford and SP4 Kelley.

Troop C Scout pilots at Pleiku during the Ia Drang campaign. Captain Gower on left, CWO Grimm on right with hat on.

FROM CAMBRIDGE TO SAIGON

★ ★ ★ ★ ★ ★

Hero and Sister to Be Reunited

A 20-year-old Cambridge war hero and his sister are looking forward with eager hope to a reunion in Saigon. Vietnam, some time in July.

Sp/4 Michael Kelley, 20, son of George and Dorothy Kelley of 134 5th st., Cambridge, has been awarded the Air Medal with two oakleaf clusters for meritorious achievement in more than 100 missions as a helicopter crew chief in support of ground forces.

His sister Joan, 28, now serving her second hitch as

Spec.-4 Mike Kelley   **Capt. Joan Kelley**

an Army nurse, will leave Ft. Sam Houston, Texas, for Vietnam in July, when

she hopes to see her brother.

Michael, who enlisted in the Army after graduation from Rindge Tech in Cambridge in 1965, is a born mechanic, according to his proud father, who says: "When he was just a kid he could take any old car apart and put it together so it would run."

Joan is a graduate of the Cambridge City Hospital School of Nursing. She is the oldest and Mike is the youngest in the Kelley family, which also includes Patricia, 25, and George.

Boston Herald news article, "Cambridge to Saigon."

Captain Joan Kelley, 8th Field Hospital, Nha Trang.

SP5 Kelley cleaned up to visit his sister, the captain.

SP5 Mike Kelley with his OH-13S Scout Recon Bird, "The Green Hornet," An Khe.

Two boys from Boston, Kelley and Burbank, at An Khe.

SP4 Walt Williams, HHT, expert commo tech.

An Khe E.M. Club, Doc Byrd, Kelley, Burbank.

NFGs arrive at Pleiku, December 3, 1966. Our replacements.

DEROS Day, Scouts Kasel, Kelley, and Gabel at Pleiku.

Going home on USAF C-141 Starlifter, Pleiku AFB.

Last duty station, Fort Hood, Texas. Kelley with UH-1H.

New UH-1H Huey of Co. B, 502nd Aviation Battalion, Fort Hood, Texas, 1967.

Noontime formation of aircraft maintenance platoon, Fort Hood, Texas, 1967. Most of these soldiers are either Vietnam veterans or new troops out of aviation school.

Kelley with his 1965 327 Super Sport, Temple Dragway.

Kelley and Ward at 1999 cav reunion, 063 crewman.

Troop C veterans visit Major Nave at Fort Benning reunion.

Funeral services for 1st Sgt. Joe Baron. Left to right: LTC. Billy Williams, SFC Walt Titchenell, MSG Mike Kelley, and LTC. Charles "Chuck" Knowlen. Troop C veterans of 1965–66.

Kelley at Vietnam Moving Wall pointing to SP5 George Gavaria's name, KIA, December 1, 1966, Phu Huu 2 Village.

that grew from 5 to 15 feet. They hung from trees and bushes and could strike at you in a second. A few managed to infiltrate our foxholes, bunkers, and sleeping bags. Not many of us guys liked snakes, including me. But we had a few who could handle them, usually the country boys and farmers.

Most of the time when we went out on recon missions, we engaged North Vietnamese regulars, especially in areas out near the Cambodian border and in Bong Son along the coast. They were very good soldiers who were very disciplined, and most would fight to the death. They were tough sons of bitches, for sure. Many were young, in their 20s or early 30s. Their officers and NCOs were good leaders and very smart. They had great tactics and, most of all, were very stealthy. They used camouflage and moved through the jungle like ghosts.

When we got into a firefight with them, they would creep up on us and try to get as close as possible so that we could not call in our gunships to beat them off. It was hard to spot them, but when we did, we laid down a heavy field of fire on them, including hand grenades. The NVA troops reminded me of the old warriors from the American Indian frontier wars, when the cavalry and mounted infantry fought battles against the Apache, Sioux, Commanche, and Kiowa tribes and neither side showed any mercy as they fought to the end. There were areas where we conducted operations that we called "Indian Country," such as out near Cambodia, all in very dense jungle where a whole NVA division could easily hide.

Sometimes when we flew out to an LZ, I would take my turn at manning the M-60D door gun and when we entered the LZ the pilots would tell us to open fire on the tree line to suppress any enemy ground fire. When they gave you these orders, you did not hesitate, you just pulled the trigger and fired, spraying the jungle with hot lead. If you captured any enemy or suspected enemy, such as Viet Cong, you had to treat them as such. You did not trust anyone. You may feel sorry for them, but you could not show them any compassion. It was strictly kill or be killed. As Civil War General Sherman once said, "War is hell." Don't get me wrong, we respected them for the warriors that they were, but the enemy's job is to kill you, so it was what it was.

Another enemy we had to contend with was malaria. A lot of us got it. One time, I was so sick that they put me in a field hospital to recover. I got so weak I couldn't stand up. Malaria causes stress on your heart, and I would still have bouts of it for years after coming home. Malaria was an equal opportunity disease. It struck all warriors, Americans, NVA, VC, ROK's, ARVN's, Australians, and all allied forces. It was a tropical disease, and if you were in the tropics, you would be exposed to it. It was also a killer disease, and some succumbed to it. The Army made us take a malaria pill every Sunday at chow. That was how we knew it was Sunday. We lost track of days and months, and you never knew what day it was until you got the pill.

We also all came down with dysentery. You knew it was coming when you got cramps in your stomach and bowels. We called it the "Hershey Squirts," as you could not hold it back. Didn't matter where you were, up in a helicopter or humping through the bush, it came out like a stream and ran down your legs and there was nothing you could do to stop it. And again, it infected the enemy as well. Living in dirty environments where bacteria thrives is going to give you dysentery. And all of us, American and Viet Infantry, were "dirt soldiers."

It's hard to remember everything in the order that it happened in. My mind is foggy and because one day was a lot like the next one, everything gets blurred together. The fog of war and time takes its toll. A few things do stand out, however. Like the time I almost drowned while crossing a swift river. We were on a recon and had to step onto wet, slippery rocks to cross the river. Somehow, I lost my footing and fell into the river, weighed down with all my gear and ammo. I sank like a rock. I tried to reach the surface but could not get up. I remember looking up and seeing the surface of the water, and then suddenly, someone grabbed me and pulled me up. I began to gasp for air and cough up water. I felt like I had to puke my guts out. The guy who saved my ass was John Cannon, a Black kid from 3rd Squad.

Cannon was a nice guy from down south and I will never forget how he saved my life. After I re-joined my squad, I was soaking wet but very much alive. I look back on that incident today and realize that Cannon should have been awarded a Soldier's Medal for saving my life. If Cannon, or any of his relatives, are reading this, I want you to know how much I appreciate what he did for me. I will never forget it.

Our recon patrols covered a lot of different terrain. One week we might be out in the coastal plains of Bong Son, sloping through a rice paddy or sweeping through a small fishing village for signs of the enemy. We almost always took sniper fire and ran into booby traps. Charlie (the enemy) was an expert in making all kinds of booby traps. He could take an empty soda can and create an explosive device that would blow your foot off or worse if you set it off. Sometimes we ran up against fortified areas. Usually, the enemy would build slit trenches along a tree line with jungle growth to cover them. Deeper into the bush, they built reinforced bunkers for their machine guns. They placed snipers up in the trees, like the Japanese did in the Pacific War, to shoot down on us.

When we ran into these things, usually under a heavy volume of fire, Captain Knowlen would call for gunship support. Our Huey gunships would come down and fire rockets and machine guns at the enemy positions and work them over pretty good. Some of the gunships were armed with the "Hog" rocket system, twin rocket pods filled with 48 2.75mm rockets each. Those could be fired in spreads of four to six rockets per volley. Some rockets had "Willie Peter" (white phosphorus) warheads on them, which were especially deadly. The phosphorus would burn the skin and create terrible wounds on the enemy troops.

Other patrols took place out along the Cambodian border near the Ho Chi Minh Trail complex, anywhere from the Ia Drang Valley up to Kontum and Dak To. Lots of steep hills and mountains out there with triple canopy jungle trees. We could walk five miles in that deep, dark shit and never see daylight. The only place we saw any was when we came across rivers and streams out there in the wilderness. Those were also good places to find the enemy. Rivers and streams were where they got their water supplies.

It was very difficult to spot the enemy in that country. Our recon Scout helicopters would fly just above the treetops looking for any sign of enemy activity. Enemy troops were told not to fire on our recon helicopters, as it would give their position away. If the Scouts did not see anything, the troop commander, Major Billy Nave, would order

Captain Knowlen to insert the Blues on the ground to conduct a ground reconnaissance. We were only a small, understrength platoon and, in most cases, we were always outnumbered. If the place was crawling with the enemy, we had to work fast.

Once contact was made, sometimes they ambushed us. We laid down a base of fire and called in the gunships to shoot them up. Division was notified of the contact and they would deploy an air assault of one or two infantry companies out to our location and take over the contact from us. Our Slicks would come out to get us and get our butts out of the firestorm. In a way, we were "duck decoys," sent out to lure the enemy to attack us, so we could make contact and call in the big infantry units to pound the crap out of them.

The helicopter war of the Air Cavalry was the most exciting and scary part of my life. I was just a teenager and had all the ammo I wanted and lots of targets to shoot at. I was doing what I wanted to do, flying in a Huey at treetop level, getting shot at, and jumping into enemy territory. It was thrilling and scary at the same time. The heat and humidity were pretty bad, but it was a hell of a lot better than freezing my ass off at Fort Dix, New Jersey. Being a part of the Aero Rifle Blues gave me all the action I wanted.

CHAPTER NINE

Aero Weapons Red Platoon

Mike

Being the new man in a combat unit is one of the worst things to be. Most of the men in the weapons platoon avoided me at first, and I felt alone in my fears. That first night in the tent they kept to themselves, sitting under the one 60-watt bulb, playing cards and smoking cigarettes. One guy, SP4 Clark, who was a short, slim man, lay on his cot, rubbing his bayonet with a stone to sharpen it. As he puffed on his cigarette, he began to joke about his last mission when he had shot a couple of NVA with his M-60 door gun. His description sent shivers down my spine.

Another soldier, a six-foot Navaho Indian they called "The Chief," got up and began to swing his arms around in a simulation of swinging his machine gun out of the back of the Huey to fire at the enemy troops.

Soon everyone in the tent was laughing loudly. I couldn't understand how these guys could laugh at killing and dying like that. Many years later, I would ask one of my old pilots about it at one of our unit reunions.

"I guess it's just how we coped with it, you know? The dangers and stresses of battle were really more than any of us were prepared to handle. Most of them were probably just as scared as you were that day, but we were more shit-scared to show it."

At some point during all the joking and laughing, "The Chief" came over to me.

"If you screw up out there, kid, I'm going to personally kick your ass!"

It was bad enough that I had to worry about being shot by the enemy, now I had to worry about this guy too. I was scared out of my mind, I didn't need some big Indian guy to make it worse. Oddly enough, "The Chief" had a mortal fear of getting shot in the ass and ironically that's what happened to him later. His wound was probably painful, but his departure ended up making my life a whole lot easier.

My first couple of days with my unit were spent working on improving the helipad, nicknamed the "Golf Course." They marched us down to the open field near the landing area and made us cut down small trees and trim back brush with hand tools. It was back-breaking work, but it was the only way to do it. They couldn't use bulldozers because they would disturb the turf and turn the camp into a dust bowl.

After what seemed like a lifetime, my platoon NCO, Esteban Guadalupe, an old-time soldier, took me down to the flight line and assigned me to a helicopter. While I was there, I observed that many of the old timers had been in either World War II or Korea. Some were veterans of both wars. Sergeant First Class Stark wore two 1st Cav patches for Korea and Vietnam.

Esteban introduced me to one of the crew chiefs, an Italian kid from Chicago by the name of George Gavaria. Unlike most of the other guys, who seemed to avoid me, George was a friendly guy. He took the time to talk to me, and even gave me a reason as to why the others were a little cold to me. He became my mentor.

"Kelley don't sweat these guys. They're ok, you know. It's just going to take them a little bit of time to warm up to you. You're coming into the platoon to replace some good friends who we lost in Ia Drang."

We talked about how most of the men in the platoon had been together since their Fort Benning days with the 11th Air Assault Division. I was an outsider, and in some cases, probably an unwanted one in the tight knit group that I had found myself in the middle of. At some point during our conversation, I realized that I was going to have to prove myself as a worthy member of the platoon if these guys were ever going to accept me.

George took the time to show me around. Later, I witnessed him helping and encouraging the others. I found a few men even went so far as to call him "Father George," as he was always dispensing kindness. George was a top-notch aircraft mechanic. Whenever I had the opportunity, I would observe his techniques for field duty maintenance on his UH-1B Huey gunship. His bird was the best maintained in our troop.

On my first day down at the flight line, my helicopter, tail number 063, was parked next to George's bird. He showed me how to pull a pre-flight inspection as well as how to fill out the aircraft logbook. SFC Guadalupe assigned a veteran crewman to teach me some on the job training (OJT) of the aircraft weapons systems and my M-60 door gun.

SP5 Walt Titchenell, a 24-year-old career Army man, showed me how to disassemble and clean the outboard quad M-60 machine-gun system called the XM-16 system, the twin rocket pods filled with 2.75-inch folding fin aerial rockets, and my hand-held M-60 7.62mm door machine gun. Walt and I would be flying together for my first combat missions.

The rest of the men in the platoon looked at me as a "cherry," meaning I was a virgin to combat. Both untested and unreliable. I was issued a flak jacket, a .45 caliber automatic pistol, a survival kit, and an M-79 grenade launcher. On a shake-down flight over the jungle a few miles outside of our base camp, I was allowed to fire my M-60 door gun to get a feeling for it. I had never seen an M-60 before Vietnam. Later in the war, the Army required all new troops to go through a pre-combat training course. But in 1965, there was no time to be giving formal classes on warfare and everything was "learn as you go."

The 1st of the 9th had participated in many battles since early October and their soldiers knew what it was like to engage in combat. In the Ia Drang operation, they had lost a gunship fighting the NVA. It had been shot down and all its crew were killed in action. The jungle had been so thick and deep that it took them weeks to locate the wreckage of the aircraft. That story stuck in the back of my mind every time I went up in my gunship.

My first big mission was during Operation *Clean House*. The troop was sent out over the Soui Ca Mountains east of An Khe, north of Highway 19, in a place the veterans called "Happy Valley." Troop C was equipped with 10 UH-1B Huey gunships. Some of the gunships had the XM-16 sub-system and some were equipped with a special rocket pod that held 48 rockets that were called "The Hog." On a routine combat mission, two gunships would fly back-up support for a Scout recon team or would go into a hot LZ to provide suppressive fires so that our infantry platoon (the Blues) could make an air assault into the LZ. We had three aero troops—A, B, and C—all equipped with a platoon of gunships, Scouts, and lifts (infantry Slicks).

Besides the three aero troops, there was a headquarters troop to provide administration, supply, medical, communications, and maintenance support. Delta Troop was a heavy weapons unit with a platoon of infantry equipped with 60 and 81mm mortars, .50 caliber M-2 machine guns, and a fleet of M-151 Ford Jeeps with either 106mm recoilless rifles or M-60 machine guns mounted on pedestals, called the "Rat Patrol." Anytime the various infantry platoons of the other troops got into a big battle, Delta Troop would provide backup supporting fire. They also performed ground patrols in the jungles and mountains.

Operation *Clean House* began on an overcast morning in mid-December. We took off for the Soui Ca area, where I would begin my OJT in combat. Instead of turning wrenches with the 15th Transportation Battalion at base camp like I had expected, I was flying at treetop level over the Gia Mang-An Khe Pass in a fully armed Huey gunship with my M-60 on my lap. I had a 100-round assault pack attached to the belt feed and the wind blowing in my face as we cruised along Highway 19 East at 80 knots. My feelings were mixed—exhilaration, fear, and excitement. My mind would sometimes flash back to the street corner where I spent all my non-productive teenage years, and I would realize that I was now in more action that I ever could have imagined.

My eyes took in the sights of the mountains and the jungle valleys while my ears took in the sounds of flight—the whine of the Lycoming jet turbine engine, the steady thumpity-thump of the rotor blades, and the radio traffic as pilots spoke with each other, with the chase ship behind us. Then, a call came in from our troop commander, Major Billy Nave, or Thirsty 6.

"Thirsty 23, this is Thirsty 6!"

"Thirsty 6 this is 23. I copy you clear."

"Thirsty 23, what is your location? Over."

"Thirsty 6, we have cleared the pass and are covering the road convoy due east."

"Roger 23. What is your ETA to the AO?"

"Ah, 6, we estimate our ETA to the CP at 0900."

"23, report your ETA to the forward CP on their freq, do you copy?"

"6, roger that. We copy. 23 out!"

The terms confused me at first, but I caught on quickly. ETA was easy, Estimated Time of Arrival. AO was area of operations, CP was for command post, and freq meant frequency. We had to keep our communications as short and cryptic as possible in case the enemy was listening in.

Lieutenant Joe Waters and Chief Warrant Officer Mike Bogdue, my pilots that day, swapped jokes about the wooden shacks they were building with the other pilots for sleeping quarters. The pilots called them hootches, and I would come to find that they were built from discarded ammunition packing cases. Some were well-designed homes, while others were barely serviceable shacks. Even the worst of the shacks was better than where we slept. The enlisted men lived in worn-out, leaky, GP medium tents down by the smelly outdoor latrine.

Our pilots were a mix of commissioned and warrant officers. Some of the warrant officers, like Mike Bogdue, had been NCOs before they were commissioned to officer rank. Many of them made the best pilots, especially those who had already completed a Vietnam tour. Then there were the pilots who were looking for trouble.

The pilots were expected to lead by example. I would later learn that they were rotated between aircraft. Sometimes you got a combination of a chief warrant officer as pilot and a captain as co-pilot. Other times, a captain would be the aircraft commander and a 2nd lieutenant would be the co-pilot. I always liked flying with the older pilots, as they were consistently cautious, steady as a rock, and reliable. They took less chances than the younger "hot dog" pilots.

During Operation *Clean House*, I was off to a good start with two of the best pilots in our troop. We flew cover for a 3rd Brigade truck convoy making its way on the dangerous, twisting road down the mountain pass.

We scouted both sides of the road, looking for signs of enemy ambushes. None were found.

The pass was a very dangerous place, especially in poor weather when fog and mist would cling to the sides of the mountain. Trying to negotiate the route could be deadly. A few trucks lost their brakes and crashed off the road, slowing up the convoy.

"What's that?" I pointed to the first of several old military vehicles along the side of the road.

"The French Army was ambushed here in the '50s by the Viet Minh. No one ever got up here to clean them up, I guess."

A bit further down the pass, the wreckage of an Air Force A-1E Sky Raider was laying off to one side of the road. I marveled at it, not knowing that I would see many aircraft meet the same fate as that of the Sky Raider during my tour of duty. We were also just a breath away from death there, and every wreckage reminded me of that fact.

We soon cleared the pass and made it down to the coastal plains on the east side of the mountains. After flying cover for the truck convoy on Highway 19, we arrived at the forward command post on the side of the road.

Our pilots brought in our birds to hover over a parking area on the south side of the road. We got out and secured the weapons systems. The pilots walked over to the tactical communications center (TOC) to find out if they had any other missions for us. A few minutes later, more aircraft from our unit arrived. We set to checking the aircraft for hydraulic leaks and cleaning our weapons.

Pop! Pop!

A noisy firefight broke out across a wide-open rice field that appeared to be about a mile away. It was exciting for me, being the first battle that I had heard.

"Looks like one of the 3rd Infantry Brigade units is engaged in a battle over there." One of the Ia Drang veterans nodded. None of the veterans were impressed by the sounds as they built up to a hot crescendo and then sputtered off. They just continued to play cards and smoke cigarettes as the action played out around us.

The radios from the TOC were crackling with urgent messages as staff officers and infantry commanders talked over the radio net. Out of the mountain pass came a loud roar. I looked up to see about 50 UH-1D Huey Slicks of the 229th Assault Helicopter Battalion flying into the valley towards the firefight. The sound of their rotors thumping the air and the long line of formation flying was majestic, and I stared at the sky in awe.

"An Eagle Flight," the veteran who had spoken before informed me.

Whatever it was, I knew it was something I would never forget.

The Slicks began to descend and turn, landing in groups near the area where the battle had been raging a few minutes earlier. *It's just like one of those old Western movies, when the cavalry rides to the rescue.* I was sucked into the excitement, not knowing I was about to be a part of it very soon.

"Get ready to take off!" our pilots shouted to us as they returned from the TOC. Titchenell, my partner in this mission, and I put the barrels back into the outboard guns and took the safety off the rocket pods.

"Ready to Rock and Roll!" Titchenell shouted.

We took off, headed towards the area where the battle had just occurred. We flew over the wide rice paddy fields, landing near the forward infantry battalion CP. The pilots shut down the aircraft and hopped out, headed towards the CP to get target information.

Not more than 20 feet away there was a well-worn dirt path leading into some high hedges and brush. I got out of the helicopter and walked up the dirt path, armed with only my .45 caliber pistol. I came to an opening in the hedges and stepped forward into an open glen. This was where the infantry had set up their CP.

This is it. This is where the action is.

Infantry soldiers were running in every direction, some carrying supplies and ammunition, others tending to some wounded men. Off to the side, I saw a pile of captured enemy equipment. Sporadic gunfire flared up again as the soldiers flushed Viet Cong from a nearby hill. With all the grunts around me, I didn't feel like I was in any danger. I was excited, seeing all the action up close like that. I walked over to the pile of captured equipment to get a closer look.

"Get lost kid!" An angry looking trooper covered in mud came up out of nowhere.

I backed away and began returning to the aircraft. As I walked back along the dirt path, I saw some soldiers herding a line of captured Viet Cong. They had on black pajama pants rolled up to their knees and no shirts. Commo wire tied around their necks linked them together, and they were all standing in about a foot of water in the rice paddy. This was my first close look at the enemy.

A Slick came in and hovered just above the rice paddy, where the soldiers were standing with the prisoners. The helicopter's skids were bobbing in and out of the water, causing tiny shock waves to ripple out over its surface. A fine spray of water went out from the rotor wash in a wide arc. The soldiers struggled with the terrified VC as they attempted to load them onto the craft. I watched our men wearily push, pull, and drag the VC closer to the waiting helicopter. Would they succeed?

I didn't get to wait around and find out.

"Kelley! Get back to the gunship, soldier!" My pilots emerged from the CP, yelling. I ran down the dirt path as fast as I could, wondering what was going to happen to the men who were captured.

We cranked up the power and took off in search of more of the enemy. The hedges below were lined with young troopers, mostly around my age, waiting to go into action. But they did not appear to be eager about it. Most of them looked lonely and scared. I could do nothing but hang out the open door and give them a thumbs–up as the helicopter flew off. The men recoiled angrily from the rotor wash that sprayed water on their faces and blew their shelter half-tents over, but a few looked up and waved back. *Those boys are going to be in the thick of that fight in just a few minutes. Some of them will be wounded or killed.* I felt a sudden wave of gratitude over how much safer I was in my gunship.

Our bird climbed out and we leveled off at around 200 feet. The pilots checked the map while discussing the mission. Titchenell leaned in towards me, indicating he, too, wanted to talk.

"Keep your gun on safe! Don't do anything until I tell you, understand?"

I gave him a weak grin. My heart beat faster as I curled my finger around the trigger. I was so scared and excited I could hardly breathe.

Titchenell lowered the green visor on his flight helmet and gave his M-60 a final check. He reached over and slapped me on my knee.

"We gonna get us some Cong today!"

That was when I started to panic. *What the hell is this crazy guy so happy about? Who in their right mind looks forward to getting shot at? Not me!*

Our gunship passed over what looked like a small village of thatch-roofed homes surrounded by tropical palm trees. People scurried about in every direction. *They look like a bunch of rabbits on hunting day.* We had orders not to open fire unless we could confirm enemy contact.

The pilots took us down on the deck at treetop level. No enemy ground fire. *So far, so good.* We cleared the village and flew out over a wide expanse of rice paddies. As we reached the end of the field, we saw eight or so men walking through some tall grass near the tree line.

"Over there!" Titchenell pointed. "Get closer! I want to check them out!"

We flew right over them and saw they were dressed in black pajama pants with khaki shirts and what looked like packs on their backs. They were not armed. We pulled up and turned in a tight circle to prepare for another pass.

"What do you think, Titchenell?" Waters steadied the craft.

"They look like Cong to me, sir. PAVN." This was short for People's Army of Vietnam.

"We can't take them under fire unless we confirm."

Just as we came around for a second pass, we came under fire from the tree line to our right.

"Looks like you were right on that call, Titchenell."

We pulled up in a steep climb and began to line up for a gun run.

Waters requested permission to open fire over the radio to our TOC. They replied, "Negative. Hold your fire!"

"We're receiving fire, now!" Then Waters opened fire with our outboard quad machine guns, blasting away at the PAVNs in the grass. They had their weapons hidden, and when we had come back for that second look, they picked them up and fired on us. The chatter of firing guns was all around us.

"What do you want me to do? Get out and ask these guys for an identity card?"

There was a long sigh over the radio from the TOC.

"Permission to fire granted."

Titchenell and the door gunners from our chase ship opened fire and peppered the grass with hot 7.62 rounds, bracketing the troops. Then we pulled up and made a run on the tree line with our 2.75-inch rockets, blasting the trees with high explosives. Through all this, Titchenell never gave me the order to fire my weapon. He was so busy shooting the targets that he forgot about me. I just sat there and watched the action. It was like a war movie, only the bullets were real. They were trying to kill us!

After we finished the gun runs, we returned to our forward CP to reload the weapons systems and top up our fuel tank. As Titchenell talked with the other crewmen about the mission, I sat quietly, listening to him tell them what happened.

It was like I was an outsider, not a part of the action. That was okay with me. I was in shock. I couldn't believe what had just happened. I had a sinking feeling in my gut as I realized that it could all happen again within a matter of minutes. And it did.

We got a new mission and took off, heading north. We flew along the left side of Highway 1, which ran along the coastline. It was a lush, tropical paradise, more like a place to build a seaside condo than to wage a war, with white sandy beaches and the beautiful, greenish-blue South China Sea. We saw some railroad tracks a little inland from the road and turned off to follow them north. We had gone about five miles when our pilots decided to turn back and check out a different area. We started to turn when a sound came from the rear of the bird.

Crack!

"We've been hit!"

The words had barely made it out of Bogdue's mouth when the Huey went into a steep turn with the craft banked over so far to the right that I became grateful for the safety harness that was barely holding me in place. Palm trees flashed by my face like pickets on a fence. We were doing around 60 knots, but we had slowed down in the turn. It was sheer pandemonium.

"Follow us for a gun run!" I heard the pilot shouting to the chase ship as we came out of the turn and lined up on the enemy. Titchenell had somehow managed to drop a white smoke marker when we had been hit and it was now billowing smoke from the palm trees near the railroad tracks. It seemed like everyone was yelling out commands above the noise of the helicopter as our gunship rapidly climbed into attack position.

"Where did that fire come from?" our pilot asked as he glanced briefly at Titchenell.

"There's a small building under the trees!" Titchenell leaned out the door and pointed towards the tracks. "Right there! Right there! Do you see them little bastards? Get closer so I can rake them!"

With the smoke as his guide, the pilot soon saw the target. Viet Cong were lining up alongside the hut as one guy passed out weapons. The pilot lined up the bird and Titchenell let go a long burst of machine-gun fire. His tracer rounds arched down into the earth, chewing up the dirt near the tracks as he walked them right up to the building, hitting the VC dead center. The enemy fell like bowling pins, like it was a Saturday night "Duck Shoot." Hot brass flew all over the aircraft cabin and burned my neck and face as pieces of it hit me. The floor of the gunship was covered in expended shell casings. The gun smoke that filled the cabin smelled good. The sweet smell of victory.

Our pilots were overjoyed at the gunner's skill. They pulled our bird up and away from the target, so our chase ship could make a run and finish off anyone who was left.

"Kelley! Fire that weapon and give us some cover!" Bogdue ordered as he piloted the bird up and away. I pointed my M-60 out the door and squeezed the trigger. It coughed out about ten rounds of fire and then jammed up. *Just my luck!* I frantically tried to unjam the weapon as we prepared to go in for a second run on the target.

"Goddamit Kelley! Get your head out of your ass! Fire that weapon!" This time it was the co-pilot who was getting mad at me.

This just added more tension to my situation. *My first combat action and my gun is screwed up, my officer is on my ass, and somewhere on the ground someone is trying to kill me.* It was not a good day for me. When we returned for the second run, hawk-eyed Titchenell had spotted some more Viet

Cong hiding in a trench under some palm trees. These were probably the ones who had taken us under fire on the first fly-by. He hung out the side door like John Wayne as the pilot slowed down the birds forward speed. Titchenell dropped some canisters of Willie Peters right over the open trench. They hit the palm trees and exploded in a white, flowery air burst, showering the Viet Cong with a nasty cloud of white phosphorous.

That was a fate worse than instant death. It was a slow death. Those poor bastards must've suffered something awful.

The pilots headed back to base, reporting our attack over the radio to the CP. Everyone was happy and excited. Titchenell rested his back against the bulkhead and let out a big smile.

"Hey boy! I told you we were gonna get us some Cong, didn't I?"

I didn't know what to say as I looked at him. I was flabbergasted.

We flew back to base at Highway 19 and landed with the other aircraft from the troop. As the pilots shut down the turbine engine and the rotors slowly turned to a stop, Chief Bogdue climbed out of the cockpit and turned to me.

"Kelley! What is wrong with you?"

"Sir? My gun jammed."

"Don't give me that shit! You froze up on me, didn't you?"

"No sir, my gun jammed."

"Bullshit!"

He walked away to the CP to file his report. I felt like I was two feet tall. There was no way to convince him of the truth, that my gun really had jammed up. George Gavaria came up shortly after we landed.

"What was that all about?"

"He says I froze, but my gun jammed. It just stopped firing. Right in the middle of my first…"

He picked up the M-60 and placed the butt stock of the gun on the floor of the gunship with the barrel facing skyward.

Bang! As soon as the butt plate bumped the floor, the live round that was still in the chamber discharged. I jumped backwards.

The noise made everyone around us come running to see what had happened, including Chief Bogdue, who was red-faced with anger when he saw what had happened.

"Dammit Kelley! What the hell are you doing discharging that weapon!"

"Sir, I…"

He cut me off in mid-sentence, chewing me out once again, but this time it was in front of everyone, including all the veterans. It seemed I was nothing but a dumbass cherry. An NFG, slang for "New Friggin Guy." Gavaria jumped in to save me.

"Sir, that was me. Kelley here was telling me how his weapon got jammed and I picked it up to inspect it. As soon as I set the butt down over here, it went off."

Bogdue looked at Gavaria like he thought he was lying. *Of course, a veteran like him would never screw up. Only the new guys screw up in the chief's mind.* Somehow, Gavaria managed to calm Bogdue down and he left with the other pilots for the CP.

Fifteen minutes later Bogdue returned with a new command pilot, Major Dick Marshall, a career Army aviator who was a combat veteran of the battle of Ia Drang Valley. It was time for another mission. We armed the guns and took off towards Happy Valley. We flew out over a lot of small coastal villages, dotted with palm trees, where we didn't see any enemy activity. Then we turned towards a vast area of rice paddies. When we flew over the farmers working there, they didn't even bother to look up, as though we were just a pesky hornet buzzing around their heads.

We kept flying, looking to the distant tree line for possible enemy fire. As we reached the end of a rice paddy with a 200 or so yard dike, a lone Vietnamese man jumped out from behind it and took us under fire.

Bogdue started yelling again.

"Cut him down Titchenell! That crazy bastard is trying to take us on!"

He's definitely right about that guy being crazy. It looked like that VC was committing suicide, the way he was standing in the open and shooting at us. Major Marshall brought the bird around in a tight turn and we made a run at him. He was still trying to hit us from 300 feet away with what looked like an automatic weapon. Titchenell opened fire with his M-60 and for a minute they were firing almost point blank at each other and nothing was happening.

Pop! Titchenell's gun stopped firing as the sound from within the cabin echoed in my ears. I turned to Titchenell and he was laying against the rear bulkhead with his flak jacket covered in bright red blood.

"I'm hit! I'm hit!"

The lone VC had got a lucky shot off. He hit the assault pack on the side of Titchenell's gun, causing the ammunition to explode and shatter shrapnel into his face, arms, and legs. His M-60 hung loose from its strap mount and dangled in the open door. Major Marshall pulled the gunship away and headed back to the CP.

"Kelley! Get the first aid kit and help him!"

I heard Bogdue yelling at me, but I was in shock and could not move. What just happened? It was like a nightmare. Only it was real.

"Dammit Kelley!" Bogdue climbed out of his seat and over the control console. "What the hell's wrong with you?"

I watched him pull the first aid kit down from the side bulkhead. He took out some bandages and began to wrap them around Titchenell's head and arm. One end of the bandage unrolled, and I watched as it flapped in a long, bloody trail in the slipstream.

"It's going to be alright, Titch. You're going to be alright."

I wasn't sure if Bogdue was trying to convince Titchenell or himself. The door gunner's face looked ashen and it appeared he was going into shock.

We got back to the CP in about 10 minutes. Major Marshall brought the gunship in for a fast landing near a medical tent with a large, red cross on its side. The rotor wash blew up a dust storm of debris and made the canvas tent billow out and flap. Two medical orderlies and a doctor ran out with a stretcher to get Titchenell. As the two orderlies ran back into the tent with him, the doctor came over to Marshall.

"God dammit, major! You almost blew my tent down!"

"Sorry doc. I just wanted to get my man to medical before it was too late."

"I have wounded men in that tent that you just blew dirt into, major!" The doctor rushed off into the tent after chewing out the major. I felt bad for him, but it was good to know I wasn't the only one making errors. *Even high-ranking soldiers make mistakes.*

Later that afternoon, I was paid a visit by SFC Guadalupe.

"I hope you learned what you needed to out there today, Kelley, because I don't have anyone else to assign to train you. From now on, you're on your own. Tomorrow you get a new door gunner and you are officially the crew chief."

My new door gunner arrived shortly after that, set up his equipment, and checked over the weapons systems. I had been told that the door gunners took care of the aircraft weapons system and the crew chief oversaw maintenance. A good team of door gunners and crew chiefs would help each other, though.

The next day we got a new pair of pilots and flew some missions up in the Happy Valley but made no contact. The valley had been worked over by elements of the 3rd Brigade and they had flushed the enemy out.

That night, after evening chow, our pilots told us to get our gear out of the gunship. We were to set up a tent on the ground and they were going to sleep in the bird. We did as we were told.

Just before dark, a tall, lanky figure walked into our camp.

"What do you boys think you're doing?" The squadron commander, Lieutenant Colonel John B. Stockton, was making his rounds of the perimeter.

"We're getting ready to get in our sleeping bags and get some rest, sir."

"This is your ship here, right?"

We looked and acknowledged him ever so slightly.

"No one sleeps in your ship but you! Pick up your gear and put it back in that ship now!"

With that said, he walked away into the closing darkness. A few minutes later, our pilots returned and picked up their gear, disappearing into the night without saying a word. The colonel had apparently informed them of the situation. I found out later that he had a reputation for taking good care of his enlisted men.

That night, we had a good laugh and a good night's sleep away from the damp, snake-infested ground. It was one of the times that made me realize that it was good to be an enlisted man in the 9th Cavalry.

CHAPTER TEN

The Bong Son Campaign

Mike

After Operation *Clean House* ended in late December, our troop returned to base camp at An Khe to refit our equipment and pull any maintenance and repairs needed before we were sent out on a new operation. The 1st Cavalry Division had three combat infantry brigades that were rotated out to the field on operations. Usually, one brigade was sent out to the Pleiku area near Cambodia, another was sent east along the South China Sea, and a third was kept at base camp as a reserve. The reserve unit was one that had just completed a major operation and needed some time in the rear to refit and resupply itself.

When a brigade was sent out on an operation, it needed a recon unit to scout ahead and screen the flanks of the infantry. That recon unit was the 1st Squadron, 9th Cavalry. The 1st of the 9th would deploy one of its troops—Alpha, Bravo, or Charlie—to a brigade to provide scouting and screening for major operations. Most of the big battles the brigades got into were initiated by Scouts from the 9th Cavalry. It was our job to go out in the jungles and mountains and search for the enemy.

Once we spotted them, we engaged them in combat and tried to hold contact until the brigade could dispatch an infantry battalion out to the battle. The 9th Cavalry was involved in every major battle that the 1st Cavalry fought in the Vietnam War.

We had been back in base camp for a week when Christmas Day arrived, and we were all looking forward to the hot Christmas meal that the cooks were preparing for us. Hot canned turkey meat, powdered potatoes, canned vegetables, and cranberry sauce. It was almost as good as back home. Especially when we had been surviving on a diet of C-rations (pre-canned foods). The mail system was backlogged for the 1st Cavalry, so we didn't receive any mail or gift packages, but we did our best to make it feel like Christmas anyway. Some of the guys made a Christmas tree that we put up in our tent.

Then New Year's came in with a big bang. Everyone on the base fired their weapons in the air for 10 whole minutes. It was like the Fourth of July!

This was in 1966. A few days later, the Viet Cong gave us their own holiday gift.

"Crump! Crump! Crump!"

At around 0300 hours, I was woken by the sound of thunder.

"Incoming!"

I had never heard this sound before, but it didn't take me long to realize it was coming from incoming mortars trying to kill us.

Everyone jumped out of their cots and ran to a bunker a few feet from our tent. We huddled together in the darkness of the shelter, listening as shells rained down on the Golf Course. It couldn't have lasted more than five minutes, but the fear and terror we all experienced in those moments would follow us for a lifetime.

The next morning, we walked down the Golf Course to inspect the damage. A couple of Hueys had their tail booms blown off and burnt to a crisp. Small craters pockmarked the ground where other rounds had missed their marks. We were told that a group of men at the 15th Maintenance Battalion had been hit by shell fragments when a mortar fell into their tent. *So much for being a wrench turner. Not even the rear base guys are safe from the enemy.* The cold fear that had gripped me since my arrival clenched tighter in my chest.

Troop C was given a mission to provide convoy security for a long line of cargo trucks leaving An Khe for Pleiku along Highway 19 West. We took off from the flight line and flew out to begin our recon and scouting. The route to Pleiku was about 20 miles and took us through some rugged and hostile country. At the end, we had to go through the Mang Yang Pass, a notoriously dangerous area for convoys, as it was one of the enemy's favorite places for ambushes.

The line of supply trucks stretched out for almost five miles. We flew at treetop height over the convoy, looking for signs of an ambush on both sides of the road. At one point, the pilot dropped our gunship down so low that we were racing along just over the rooftops of the cargo trucks. We were cruising along at about 80 knots when we came to a hill. We pulled up just as a truck was cresting the hill and our skids almost hit his roof. *He must think we're crazy for being so low.*

We later learned that this mission was called Operation *Matador*. To us, it was just another day of flying.

When we finished our escort patrol, we landed at Pleiku Air Base and went into the snack bar to get a cold drink and something to eat. Pleiku was huge, and unlike the crude "tent city" that we lived in at the An Khe Base Camp in so many ways. There were rows upon rows of wooden barracks and maintenance hangars. And best of all, they had a well-stocked snack bar that sold hot food like hamburgers and hot dogs. A rare treat for us that was unheard of at An Khe.

We wolfed down a few hot dogs and cold drinks before returning to our gunships and heading back to base. *Man, those Air Force guys sure do live differently than the Army.* We were strictly "dirt soldiers," living in the boonies with the infantry and eating cans of pre-cooked food.

On the flight back to An Khe, we were cruising along at about 100 feet above Highway 19 with our chase ship behind us. There was light traffic on the road, and no problems ahead of us that we could see. Off to our left, about a quarter of a mile away, a large CH-54 Skycrane heavy lift helicopter was heading back to An Khe from Pleiku as well. It passed us, making good time with two huge jet turbine engines that gave it a lot of power. With my stomach full of good food, it felt momentarily serene.

Boom!

About a thousand feet in front of us, the Skycrane exploded in a massive fireball and plummeted to the ground. Black smoke billowed from the jungle floor where it had impacted. Our pilot immediately got on the radio to notify An Khe of the accident.

"Fly over that site and see if there are any survivors. You want to get them before the enemy does!" our orders crackled back, and I was jerked back into the reality of where I was so suddenly that the hot dogs became a rock in my stomach, no longer such a pleasant memory.

We banked left, dropped to treetop level, and made a couple of passes over the burning wreckage to see if there was anyone still alive. Then the pilot brought our ship in to hover above the wreckage, drifting from side to side, looking at the jungle floor. Trees had been cut down and burned from the crash and a large crater had appeared, filled with the broken parts of the CH-54. We could see the center and rear of the fuselage and a body in the rear compartment, most likely that of the crane operator. Hundreds of pages from an Army technical manual had been scattered around, some clinging to the trees like white leaves. There were no survivors.

I didn't get as much time to ponder the suddenness of it all as I would have liked, although maybe that was a good thing.

On January 25, 1966, we got ready to take off on a new operation, Operation *Masher-White Wing*. The tactical plan involved moving 1st Cavalry Brigade Units east to a place called Phu Cat, along the coast. Phu Cat was to be a staging area for the cav to then proceed north into Bong Son, in the Binh Dinh province, to engage the North Vietnamese Army's 3rd Yellow Star Division.

That was a bad day to start a war. It was raining, and a misty fog clung low to the mountains, which was poor and dangerous flying weather. SFC Guadalupe gave me a new door gunner for the mission, PFC Hosie Ward, a 19-year-old kid from Washington, D.C. Hosie was an NFG just like me. So now we had a completely green enlisted crew.

We took off into the low cloud ceiling and headed out to the An Khe Pass to fly cover for the truck convoys heading east to Phu Cat. When we arrived, traffic was held up due to an aircraft accident. An Air Force C-123 transport that had been loaded with troopers from the 2/7th Gary Owen Battalion, many of whom were veterans of Ia Drang, had crashed into the mountain in the fog. The wreckage was strewn all over the road as convoy soldiers tried to pull the dead and injured from the remains of the plane. I was filled with sadness as I watched the plumes of smoke still drifting from the wreckage.

By the time we completed flying security over the convoy, the fog had burned off and the sun came out. We arrived at the Phu Cat airstrip and parked our bird a few hundred feet away from the active runway. The place was buzzing with activity. Air Force cargo planes landed and took off rapidly, discharging supplies and troops to support the new operation. Long lines of Army cargo trucks were being loaded with the supplies and then moving out to a staging area north of the airstrip near coastal Highway 1. We hung around our gunship, writing letters and eating our C-rations. There were no more missions that day, and by 1600 hours the rest of Troop C's aircraft arrived at our new base at Phu Cat.

The next day we prepared the ship for the day's missions while eating hot powdered eggs and rubbery bacon. By 0900 hours we were airborne and headed towards some mountains off to the northwest. On this mission, we had new pilots. Chief Warrant Officer Leonard "Pappy" Green, and a brand-new 2nd Lieutenant, Richard Mehan. Chief Green was a good-natured older pilot with a solid flight record. Lieutenant Mehan had his minimum required flight hours, but it wouldn't be long before he racked up a lot of airtime flying missions with the troop.

This time we flew as the chase ship behind our troop commander's aircraft. Major Nave led us up into some rugged foothills, a thickly jungled area with no open spaces to drop our Blues into. We dropped to treetop level, cruising along at a slow 40 knots, trying to spot any enemy activity on the jungle floor. Often, we would spot a well-worn footpath or a string of black commo wire threading through the trees and bushes along the trail. Other times, our only sign of enemy activity occurred when the enemy took us under fire.

That's exactly what happened as we flew over a ridgeline.

"It sounds like automatic weapons fire!" Green shouted as Major Nave's crew chief lobbed a white smoke canister onto the ridge from the ship in front of us. The white smoke billowed up through the trees and drifted skyward. Our gunships wheeled around in a tight turn and we made a pass over the smoke, firing our door guns into the jungle. Major Nave brought his bird to a hover right over the smoke and his gunners poured hot 7.62 fire into the jungle where we thought the enemy was located. The jungle was so thick, it was impossible to see anything on the ground. We knew the enemy was down there, but we could not see them.

After a minute or so, we pulled away from the area. Major Nave got on the radio to request an artillery strike and we hightailed it out of there before the big guns opened fire. Flying around in an area under artillery fire was not a good idea.

We spent the next few days flying back into those mountains and over some of the valleys that ran between them, looking for signs of enemy activity. We didn't know it at the time, but our missions northwest of Phu Cat were part of a well-planned diversion operation by the 1st Cavalry Division. The plan was to throw the enemy off our true intention, a major thrust north into the heart of the Bong Son Plains and the mountains north and west of Bong Son.

On the morning of January 28, Operation *Masher-White Wing* was officially launched by the 1st Cavalry and Troop C's aircraft were in the vanguard of the attack. It was a drizzly, misty start as we took off from Phu Cat and headed north over Highway 1, later to be known as "The Street without Joy" from a Bernard Fall book about the war. We flew low-level cover for the convoys moving into Bong Son, screening the flanks for signs of enemy ambushes. We passed over a lot of small coastal villages where people stood under the cover of lush palm trees, watching the convoy go by. I later learned that these people had not seen foreign troops in their area since the French had been there in 1954, over ten years prior.

We flew over a village where a group of young girls were washing clothes in the Bong Son River. Our pilots made a tight turn and came back over the girls to get a better look at them. As we hovered above them, they looked up, smiling and waving. That was the highlight of our day.

By late afternoon, the low, overcast sky finally did what it had been promising to do all day and the clouds opened up with heavy rainfall. We landed at our new forward base up on a plateau called LZ DOG (Landing Zone DOG). Combat engineers bustled around, busily building roads and firing positions for the artillery. Long strands of concertina barbed wire were laid out along the outer perimeter of the LZ. We set down near a graveyard and a farmer's house, and slid the doors closed to keep the rain from blowing inside our ship. It was a time for rest.

We opened up some C-rations, ate, and smoked a few cigarettes. All our aircraft were grounded. We may have been in the middle of a raging war, but at that moment, we were relaxed, dry and cozy inside our bird.

When the rain let up for a minute, I climbed out of the gunship to attend to nature's call. As I walked back to the ship, I examined the unusual grave markers. I stopped at one that caught my eye and noticed something sticking out of the ground by my feet. I bent down to pull what appeared to be a large piece of metal out of the dirt. I rubbed the crusted red soil away to reveal a chunk of an old "Pineapple" hand grenade from World War II. Excited, I looked around to see if there was more. A few feet away, another chunk of metal turned out to be a section of an artillery shell, with threads running through one side. I brought my find over to the pilots.

"Probably just pieces of shrapnel left over from when the French Army was here back in the early 50s." Green was far less enthusiastic about my discovery than I was.

I packed my war prizes into my rucksack for safe keeping. I always loved military history as a boy and I had a special fondness for World War II, so these items were meaningful to me. The thought of the shrapnel the 1st Cavalry would leave behind on these same grounds after the Bong Son campaign did not occur to me at the time.

We sat around for about another hour before the side door to our bird slid open and two very wet soldiers climbed into the back cabin to sit on the troop seat. I recognized them as CWO Jerry Grimm, a Scout pilot, and his enlisted observer, PFC Richard Gable.

"Our helicopter just got shot down near the coast." Grimm wiped rainwater off his face as well as he could with his wet sleeve. "There's a big battle going down over by LZ 4 right now."

Green handed each of the men a dry cloth as they recounted what they had seen.

"Third Brigade has a battalion of infantry engaged in a firefight with the 3rd NVA. Our bird went down near a company of the brigade's infantry and we were lucky to be rescued before the NVA could get to us."

We handed the two men a cigarette and sat in silence, pondering their luck, hoping we would have the same if we got shot down. Hoping for better luck to not get shot down in the first place.

"Well, I guess we better go file a report with the command post." Grimm opened the door and flicked his cigarette out into the pouring rain outside. "Thanks, fellas."

And then they were gone.

It continued to rain throughout the rest of the night. We stayed inside the bird, trying to get what sleep we could. But it's hard to sleep when you know there is a battle raging on all around you, and that you will be in it yourself soon. That your bird could be the next to go down.

The next morning the rain stopped, but the ceiling was still low. Huge, misty clouds hung over the LZ like a gray blanket. Despite this, my door gunner, PFC Ward, and I began to prepare the ship for action. He got the weapons systems cleaned and checked, and I went over the pre-flight inspection and checked all the fluid levels. Just after breakfast, at the field mess tent, we were told to stand by for a mission.

In a few minutes, our pilots arrived and began to get ready to fly. This time we had Captain James Kidd as our aircraft commander. Kidd was a seasoned aviator with a closely cropped crew cut, and was also the platoon leader of the weapons platoon. Richard Mehan, our friend the new lieutenant, was his co-pilot.

Crew members had to paint their helmets black, but Mehan had been sent out to the field so quickly that his helmet was still white. Like a big, white bullseye.

I liked Mehan. He was an easy-going, soft-spoken guy who was about 23 or so, not much older than me. And he had something I had always wanted. Paratroop wings. In his short Army career, he had already completed officer's training, airborne school, and flight school. He was a good man, and I knew he would make a good major someday.

We took off, heading west toward the lower end of the An Lao Valley. The mist clung to the sides of the mountains and the valleys looked spooky. We hooked up with a Forward Air Control (FAC) pilot who was flying in an 0-1 Bird Dog single engine spotter plane. He led us into a wide, heavily jungled valley and flew up at about 200 feet while we flew down to treetop level, doing a close up recon of the terrain. As usual, we were looking for any signs of the NVA and VC.

After about 45 minutes had passed and we didn't see anything, we bid farewell to the FAC and returned to LZ Dog to refuel. A short time after, our pilots came running back towards our gunship from wherever they had been during the refuel.

"Mount up! Now!" Captain Kidd swung himself into the pilot's seat. "This is a Red Alert! Get your ass in gear!"

We armed the guns and tubes, climbed aboard, and strapped ourselves in. Our M-60s were locked, loaded, and ready for action.

We took off and rapidly climbed to about 200 feet. We flew northeast to the upper end of the An Lao Valley to a high mountain range that was socked in with low fog. *I don't see how we can ever get safely through all of that.* The entrance to the valley was blocked by the mist but Captain Kidd was determined to get through. He brought our bird to a hover along the side of the mountain and slowly began to inch forward up the side. Ward and I looked out the door to see the jungle's tree tops just a few feet below us. The wall of fog began to close in around the ship.

My mouth got dry and my heart thumped heavily in my chest. I looked to Ward, and it was easy to see he felt the same way. This was a bad place to be. Our rotor blades churned the mist like a kitchen mixer beating a bowl of cream. There was no way to tell how close we were to the mountain.

I looked over to Captain Kidd to see if he looked worried. He was calm and steady. A rock in the storm. Our lives were in his hands. *I hope he knows what he's doing.* We were now faced with two enemies trying to kill us. The enemy below us in the jungle, and the weather.

After what seemed like an eternity, we finally broke through the fog into the green, misty valley on the other side. As we did, a voice came over the radio.

"Please help! Somebody please help me. I think all my men are dead, and I'm surrounded. Please help! They're all around me! My men... they're all dead! Please...help..."

"Delta Team, this is Thirsty Red, do you copy?" I was awed by how professional and calm Captain Kidd was considering what we had just been through and what was likely ahead of us.

"Thirsty Red! Thirsty Red, all my men are dead, and I am surrounded! Please get us out of here!"

"Take it easy son. We're on our way. Hold on just a little bit more, we are coming to help you."

An Air Force FAC pilot flying a Bird Dog with the call sign Robin One came to meet us as we flew into the valley. He directed us to where the Special Forces B-52 Team Capitol detachment was located on the side of the mountain. Visibility was less than a quarter of a mile and there was a very low ceiling. *These are the most dangerous flying conditions I have ever seen.* I looked to Captain Kidd for reassurance as he got on the radio. Enemy small arms fire began to crackle below us.

"We're going to make a gun run on those VC closing in on you first! Delta! Mark your position with smoke! We're coming in!"

A moment later, a cloud of red smoke billowed up from the mountainside and drifted up towards the low-hanging fog.

"Thirsty Red, put your ordinance 50 meters around my position!"

"Roger Delta, here we come!"

Kidd rolled our bird into a tight turn and lined the gun sights up with the red smoke. We went into a slow dive and Kidd opened fire with our outboard quad machine guns. The rapid fire and noise of those guns was fearsome. We saturated the ground with hot 7.62mm rounds. Then Ward and I opened fire with our door guns, spraying the area outside the smoke. As we pulled out of the attack our chase ship came in behind us, giving the area another blast of machine-gun fire. "The Green Beret wants you to make a second run, this time come right over the middle of his position!" Now it was the FAC's voice on the radio.

"Robin One, tell Delta we are making our second run. Take cover!"

"Roger Thirsty Red. Will do!"

Kidd lined us up for a second pass. We dove down and blasted the area all around the red smoke. As we pulled up, Ward and I opened fire, spraying about sixty rounds. Then our chase ship came in, following suit.

"Tell them to hold off on those door guns! Those bullets are ricocheting off rocks near my position and I am wounded."

At this point the enemy had backed away from Delta Team. They began to fire at our helicopters. Captain Kidd was not impressed by this sign of resistance. We flew around the valley in an aerial ballet, trying to avoid hitting the side of the mountains and having a mid-air crash with the FAC.

"CP, this is Thirsty Red! The situation is becoming critical. We need to mount a rescue for the Delta Team right away!"

Now low on fuel and our ammo expended, we had to leave the valley.

I later discovered that the 3rd Brigade was supposed to have a reserve rifle company on standby to help the Delta Team if it got into trouble, but the company had been committed to the big battle at LZ 4 along the coast. So their commander, Colonel Hal Moore, had called our new commander, LTC Robert M. Shoemaker, to ask him if he could mount a rescue operation. Colonel Shoemaker dispatched our gunships and ordered a rifle platoon from Delta Troop to load up on some Huey Slicks to fly out to the valley to rescue the surviving Green Berets.

After we left, Shoemaker sent in more gunships with the rifle platoon. He flew his command Huey into the valley and hovered over Delta Team, directing his rifle platoon to their position. Of the six-man recon team, only two survived, SFC Webber, and SSG Hiner, who received a head wound from our ricocheting bullets.

Years later, Hiner would reflect on this experience as the worst he ever had in his three combat tours of Vietnam. The team was rushed into the valley without the benefit of preparation and orientation. They had no reaction team to back them up, and their radio gear was not up to the task of a long mission in mountainous terrain. SFC Webber and SSG Hiner were very brave soldiers. They would never forget their harrowing patrol, deep in the Valley of Death.

We returned to LZ Dog to re-arm and re-fuel. The events of the rescue mission were quickly overshadowed by the news that we had lost one of our own, a Scout on low-level recon patrol. PFC William C. Geis, a 20-year-old kid from Chicago, had been flying as an observer with Lieutenant Robert Young when their OH-13S was shot down by NVA groundfire. They were rescued and taken to the 85th Evacuation Hospital down in Qui Nhon. We learned that Geis had died from his injuries and Young was in critical condition.

Major Marshall took our gunship down to the Qui Nhon Air Base where he and the co-pilot visited Young in the hospital. PFC Ward and I waited near our gunship, which was parked on the Air Force flight line. We watched A1E Skyraiders take off on missions, loaded with bombs and rockets. The roar of the Skyraider's radial engine reminded me of the old CH-21 Shawnees back at Davison Army Field in Virginia. The Skyraiders were awesome.

The pace of operations for *Masher White-Wing* increased over the next few days as the weather improved. We began to fly more recon and fire support missions throughout the Bong Son area. On one of those missions, we went out to a mountain range to inspect the impact area of a B-52 Arc Light bombing strike. We flew low-level over ridges that had been blasted by 500-pound bombs. There were craters as large as tractor-trailer trucks. Trees had been uprooted and thrown hundreds of feet, laying on their sides.

The Blues, our infantry platoon, had been inserted on the ground for a close-up visual recon. Their platoon leader, Captain Charles Knowlen, was in charge of relaying what they found to our pilots over the radio.

"There's dead NVA inside all the caves on this mountain. Must've been the concussion from the blasts. Those B-52s sure do good work."

When the Blues returned to LZ Dog they had a bounty of booty that they had taken from the dead NVA that included captured weapons, backpacks, bags of ammunition, and a very prized item—NVA belt buckles.

In between flights, we pulled what were called intermediate inspections of the gunship. Every 25 flight hours the aircraft was supposed to be grounded so its filters and components could be inspected. But the operations were occurring at such a rapid pace that the flight hours racked up fast. We couldn't ground the birds because they had to be mission ready. So, whenever we were on the ground between missions, we pulled a portion of the required inspections and logged the work in the aircraft logbook. This was war and you had to bend the regulations.

Sometimes a technical inspector from our maintenance section would inspect our work and write an entry in the logbook to approve it and release the bird for flight. Our gunships were living out in the field with the infantry, and they took a beating from the long flight days and the dust and dirt of field duty. There was also the weather, which ranged from cool and misty mornings to hot and humid afternoons. At times the humidity kept a helicopter from taking off if it was fully loaded, and occasionally mechanical problems would hamper a bird's flight.

One afternoon, we took off with a full load of fuel and ammunition. The co-pilot was flying, and when we lifted off and cleared the perimeter wire, the aircraft began to shudder. Suddenly, we began to lose airspeed and dropped down toward the trees on the side of the hill. *We're going to crash into the jungle!*

"Let go of the controls! Let me take over!" Our aircraft commander, CWO Frank Hiser, was an ex-Navy jet fighter pilot. The co-pilot was frozen on the collective control and didn't respond. Hiser reached over and issued a judo chop to his wrist, forcing the co-pilot to let go. Then he grabbed the controls and pushed the cyclic stick forward, dropping the nose of the airship down. I watched as he wrestled with the collective and flew down the hill, just over the top of the trees. *Please let us live.* As we slipped forward and downward, Hiser got the ship under control and slowly gained altitude as we got our airspeed back.

It was a close call, but we managed to complete our mission and return to LZ DOG.

Life on the ground at our forward base was as exciting as flying on combat patrols. Late one night, I was sleeping in my gunship when the perimeter was probed by an enemy force. Machine guns began to fire, and flares were shot from mortars, lighting up the night.

My ship was parked just a few feet from the perimeter. *If I try to make it back to the troops down the hill, some nervous security guard might end up shooting me.* I decided to hold my ground and hope for the best. I took my M-60 door gun out of the ship and laid it on the ground, aiming it toward the perimeter. I got out a box of ammunition, loaded a belt into the gun, and laid next to it, waiting for an enemy assault through the wire. As the flares flickered above me and dark shadows creeped across the trees in front of me, my heart pounded, and my mouth dried out. *Here I am, a helicopter door gunner, about to get killed defending the perimeter.*

After what seemed like hours, the probing action moved away, shifting towards the right side of my location. After about another hour of sporadic firing along the perimeter, it finally quieted down. I put the machine gun back inside the ship and climbed in to try to get some sleep. I chambered a round in my .45 and placed the safety on. That gun stayed next to my head all night as I slipped in and out of a nervous sleep.

The next morning, as dawn broke, the door to my gunship slid open. I jumped up with the .45 in my hand and pointed it at old SFC Guadalupe, putting it a few inches away from his face.

"Take it easy Kelley! Put that damn thing away!"

"Sorry, sergeant. I got caught in the middle of that perimeter attack last night. I didn't sleep much. That door opened up and I thought you might be an enemy sapper."

"You know, it might be a good idea if you took your sleeping gear and moved down the hill. Sleep in your pup tent instead of sleeping here in your ship right next to the wire."

I took his advice and pitched a tent down the hill with the rest of the troops that night. Ward had already done the same thing, and we sat under a star-filled sky, talking about our lives back home.

Around midnight, the sound of a firefight echoed across the valley from a mountain about five miles away. A few minutes later, the drone of a propeller-powered aircraft came closer to our location, but we couldn't see where it was in the darkness. Suddenly, a long, red arc of fire shot out of the darkness above us, followed by the sound of a rapid-firing gun that sounded like a buzz saw. Red tracers bounced off the mountain and it began to look like a Chinese holiday with fireworks. The sound of propellers made me think of World War II.

We found out later that this airplane was a USAF AC-47 gunship called Spooky. It was equipped with rapid fire mini-guns and was part of the 4th Air Commando Squadron. It was an amazing experience to see this gunship in action.

Another time, we watched USAF B-57 Canberra fighter bombers drop napalm canisters on the same mountain. They came in at a low-level, released their silver tanks, and then pulled straight up with their afterburners giving them extra thrust to climb away from the blast below. Red and yellow flames scorched the jungle as a huge cloud of black smoke rose skyward.

The workhorse of the Air Force, and a good friend to the 1st Cavalry Division, was the fleet of C-123 and C-130 cargo planes that brought in vital supplies to our bases and flew out soldiers going on their out-country R&R leaves to Hong Kong and Japan. The Air Force and the Army worked well together, and many battles were won based on that cooperation and mutual support. The Air Force had our back and we appreciated that, even if they had better snack bars and mess halls than we did.

We had Air Force detachments assigned to the 1st Cavalry, which consisted of weather station specialists, cargo supply technicians, fuel specialists, and an air liaison who handled operations with the FACs. These were the only Air Force personnel authorized to wear the 1st Cavalry shoulder patch, a source of pride to the airmen involved.

The missions began to blur together after a while because there were so many of them.

We flew into a coastal fishing village one time where the troop's aircraft had taken ground fire the previous day. We didn't see anything after a low-level recon, so we inserted our Blues into the area. The Blues came across a couple of Vietnamese in a rice paddy that they decided to take in for interrogation. As they lifted off, the VC opened fire on their helicopters from a nearby tree line. We rolled in for a rocket and machine-gun run as the Blues flew away with the prisoners. This was later called Operation *Snatch*.

The next day, we returned with a photographer from Division Intelligence in our bird. He had a special camera that was designed to take aerial photographs of the terrain. We made a couple of passes over the village at 200 feet. I looked down at the jump seat where he had an open case of film and noticed that the boxes were from the Polaroid corporation. *They're located back home, in Cambridge.* Here I was in the middle of nowhere, thousands of miles from home, with these boxes from home sitting right next to me. *How ironic.*

The local VC, elements of the 2nd VC Regiment, took us under fire. My pilot banked the gunship to the right and I leaned out of the door, firing my M-60 at the enemy. I pumped about 100 rounds into the trees. The photographer had never seen a firefight before.

"This is so exciting!" He fumbled for his camera, but the action was over before he could fully react. It reminded me of my first mission.

He must have had quite a story for his friends when he returned to division headquarters.

Later that afternoon, Major Nave flew his gunship into the same coastal village. They were shot down. The bird crashed, but the crew was rescued by Captain Kidd's Huey and taken back to LZ DOG. Later, a big 228th AHB CH-47 Chinook brought the ship back to DOG.

By this time, PFC Ward and I were no longer considered to be NFGs. We had about 100 combat missions under our belts and we had been accepted by the veterans as members of their "elite" team. We enjoyed our new status as combat veterans, but we still got scared when we went out on missions. Each day was just like every other, and I knew it was only a matter of time before I got hit. I woke up each morning not knowing if I was going to live or die. Often, I wished for a wound, something that wouldn't kill me but still allow me to escape the hell of combat. Out in the jungle was a NVA or VC with a bullet with my name on it.

On one mission, I was put with a young, hot shot aviator named WO Gerald Golden. We were preparing the equipment to go out on some low-level patrols over an area known as the "free fire zone" in the Bong Son area.

"Go over to the ammo bunker, Kelley, and get us some WP grenades."

"We aren't supposed to carry those anymore. The commander put the order out after Geis and Young were injured when their Scout OH-13 was shot down."

"Ah, don't worry about that. We need them. Just go get them for me."

I couldn't argue. I brought him a metal ammo box full of WP grenades. We took off, headed towards An Lao valley. Golden leaned out of his window and dropped several of those grenades on some thatched-roof buildings on a low pass. He was a good shot and the buildings caught fire and quickly burned. *So much for orders.*

After that, we were sent back to where Nave's ship had been shot down. This was a hot area. Division Artillery laid down a barrage of 105mm shells into the tree line that we had received groundfire from. The Blues Rifle Platoon was to be airlifted out to the village by our aero lift platoon of UH-1D Huey Slicks. As gunships, we were ordered to go in and provide suppressive fires around the LZ. We fired rockets and machine guns. On a couple of passes, we were on target. The Blues went in and quickly dismounted from the Slicks as they deployed into the village. There was a brief firefight before the Blues captured some VC from the 2nd Regiment.

We took heavy groundfire from the tree line that had been hit earlier by the artillery field strike. Enemy fire hit our main rotor blades and the engine compartment where a round had cut into the compressor line. We flew back to DOG and replaced the compressor line. There were no blades there, so we had to return to An Khe to get a new set at the 15th Maintenance Battalion. While there, we had a new rocket pod system mounted on our gunship. The new pods held 19 rockets each. They were actually designed for the fixed wing Mohawk aircraft, not Hueys.

We flew out to the jungle north of An Khe to test out our new equipment. Our pilots fired the rockets and our bird lurched to the right. It almost spun around as one of the pods got loose and fell off the bird, dropping 200 feet into the jungle. That scared the hell out of us.

We returned to base and got rigged up with a replacement pod. They rewired the system and then we went back out for another test run. This time, all systems worked well. We were released for duty and returned back to LZ DOG to rejoin the rest of Charlie Troop.

After the 1st of the 9th completed its recon mission and confirmed that the 2nd VC Regiment was there, division headquarters deployed elements of the 3rd Brigade's rifle companies into the village on a search and destroy operation. They found a cache of enemy weapons and supplies.

This was an operational tactic that worked well. The 9th Cavalry would go in to recon possible enemy locations, which was followed by a larger infantry brigade sweep. We forced the enemy to withdraw and regroup on many occasions. The Division Artillery played a key role in almost all of these operations by destroying enemy formations.

The combination of air mobility with helicopters and supporting fire was a good system for jungle warfare. Our division commanders, Major Generals Harry O. Kinnard and John Norton, were highly skilled in air mobility operations. They spent many years training and planning air mobile warfare, even though they were new in putting their knowledge to use in Vietnam.

CHAPTER ELEVEN

The Crow's Foot Battle

Mike

Of all my missions in the Bong Son campaign, the battle at Crow's Foot will always stand out above the rest as the most dangerous and exciting. We were sent into the Kim Son Valley southwest of LZ DOG on February 13, 1966. It was a good flying day. The sun was out, and visibility was excellent. The valley was in a rugged area with a series of mountains that sent out ridgeline tributaries down towards the valley floor; they looked like the claws of an eagle from the air, so we all called this area the Eagle's Claw and the Crow's Foot. Division Headquarters also called the area the Iron Triangle.

We were sent to fly low-level recon over the mountains to look for signs of enemy activity. The area was heavily forested, so this was not an easy task. An entire Army regiment could hide in there, undetected by our recon Scouts. We looked around the mountains and found nothing. When our fuel got low, we returned to LZ DOG to await our next mission.

After the recon from the sky, Lieutenant Colonel Robert M. Shoemaker, the 1st of the 9th Cavalry commander, deployed the Blues of Charlie and Delta Troops into the valley to perform a ground recon patrol. According to Operations Order Number 2-66 Eagles Claw, the rifle platoon of Charlie Troop (Captain Chuck Knowlen—"Thirsty Blue") was to conduct a patrol of the lower valley, while Delta Troop Blues would be inserted into the top of a ridgeline at LZ FRITZ.

The UH-1D Huey Slicks of the aero rifle lift platoon started flying the Delta Blues to LZ FRITZ at around 1200 hours. The Blues were to sweep down the ridge lines and force any enemy down the mountainside and into the valley, where the Blues of Charlie Troop would block their escape.

The top of the ridge was only wide enough for a single Slick to dismount its infantry squad. Lead pilots Chief Warrant Officers Jim Reid and Darwin Heffner hovered their ship at the top of the mountainside, fighting crosswinds. The right skid was touching the side of the mountain and the left skid was out in the air. The Blues, loaded down with rucksacks, extra canteens, ammo, grenades, radios, and other equipment, had to drop to the ground out of the right side of the bird. The downward slope of the mountain made it difficult for them to get to their feet, and the pilots later told us that some of them fell and rolled a few feet before getting their balance.

Years later, I had the opportunity to speak to two of the men who were there that day, SP4 Hector Aviles, who was one of the Delta Blues, and Pilot CWO Darwin Heffner.

Aviles remembered preparing to make the jump to the ground as a particularly harrowing experience. "When the bird came in towards the LZ, we got out on the slippery skids and balanced ourselves, praying that we did not get shot and fall off the skids, as a fall from the aircraft could be fatal."

Heffner remembered the difficulties he experienced trying to control the helicopter. "The crosswinds and updrafts were trying to blow our helicopter off the mountain, but as each ship came into the LZ, my fellow pilots skillfully manhandled their aircraft like a bucking bronco, allowing their riflemen to jump on target."

As the first bird flew out of the LZ, the next one came in, each offloading troops in a similar manner. Once Delta Troop was on the ground, they began to sweep down the ridgeline toward a hill covered in tall, thick elephant grass. Their platoon leader, Captain Fritz, deployed his troops towards the hill.

"We moved down the ridge about 100 meters or so when all of a sudden, all hell broke loose," Sergeant Larry Banks of the 3rd Platoon later recounted to me. "Heavy machine-gun fire came from the elephant grass on the hill. The enemy was well hidden in a complex of bunkers and spider holes."

Sergeant Banks and his squad began to throw hand grenades up onto the hill, but enemy fire had already begun to find soft flesh and the casualties began to mount. Delta Troop began returning fire towards the concealed enemy bunkers.

Captain Fritz looked around for one of his RTOs to call in for backup and supporting fire. His RTO was dead, and the radio had been destroyed by machine-gun fire. One of his squad leaders managed to use his RTO's radio to call in a situation report (SITREP) to squadron headquarters. He told the operations officer, Major Billie Williams, that the platoon was pinned down by enemy fire.

Major Williams sprang into action, advising LTC Shoemaker on the situation before contacting his troop commanders to organize a relief force to assist Delta Troop. All available gunships were ordered to fly into the Kim Son Valley, including my bird, 063.

About 12 gunships from the 1st of the 9th arrived on station in the valley by late afternoon. Major Williams had arranged for the aero rifle lift platoon to pick up the Charlie Troop Blues in the valley and fly them up to the top of the mountain to LZ FRITZ. Captain Charles Knowlen of Troop C Blues was in charge of the platoon on the valley floor. He recalled:

> We had been sweeping the valley with a two-fold mission: conduct a search for a stolen Army of South Vietnam (ARVN) 105mm cannon, and establish a blocking position at the lower end of the mountain. We were humping through the jungle, fulfilling the mission on what was a very hot and humid afternoon. We heard the firefight and had just enough time to wonder about what was going on before the radio began to crackle with Delta Troop's urgent messages to headquarters. Then, Major Billy Nave, the troop commander, called me.

"Thirsty Blue, this is Thirsty Six!"

Captain Knowlen took the handset from his RTO, SP4 Jerry "Smoky" Schmotolocha.

"Thirsty Six, this is Thirsty Blue!"

"Thirsty Blue, prepare for immediate extraction to assist Delta. Mark your position with yellow smoke. ETA of your lift in zero one five. Do you copy?

"Roger Six, I copy clear. Lift in zero one five. Out!"

Captain Knowlen knew they would be going into action very quickly:

> From where we were in the valley, we could hear the sounds of the battle and knew Delta had run into a hornet's nest up there.

Up on the mountaintop LZ, things were going badly for Delta Troop. The battle was turning into a meat grinder as men were shot or hit with shrapnel, and the air was filled with the noise and smoke of combat. The aero lift platoon Slicks picked up the Blues of Charlie Troop and shuttled them to the top of the mountain. SP4 Dick Timmons of the Aero Rifle Platoon recollected how:

> We came in on final approach and gunfire came up from below. Delta Blues were in heavy contact, and the whole area was full of smoke and tracer rounds from everywhere. I opened fire with my M-60. I got hit in the leg and the upper body. I kept firing until my gun jammed up.

SP4 Schmotolocha, RTO, remembered that:

> Our captain was a dam' good leader. He calmly deployed our infantry squads into attack positions. As we moved down the ridge, we came to a large anthill in the center. Captain Knowlen sent 1st and 2nd Squads to the right and 3rd and 4th Squads to the left of the anthill. Then we moved forward in a wedge formation. We began taking heavy fire from machine-gun bunkers in the tall elephant grass on the hill to our front. We took cover as best we could.

Whilst SP4 Bill "Woody" Woodward, RTO of 1st Squad, looked back on how:

> Captain Fritz started waving with his .45 and yelling at me to bring his radio over to him. Before I could react, a sniper shot me in the chest and I went down.

Right about then, Captain Knowlen assumed command of the battle. On the right flank, SP4 Gary Massey checked on Woody before collecting his hand grenades to charge up the hill into the elephant grass to get the bastard who had shot Woody. Massey took out the enemy sniper and a machine-gun bunker with the grenades. When he returned to Woody's side, Schmotolocha treated him for an arm wound. Massey was later awarded a Silver Star for Valor for his actions on the field that day.

Major Williams began to rally all of his available resources towards the fight. The 9th Cavalry had found the enemy. Now it had to lock onto them and hold the contact until the brigade could commit their infantry battalions into the valley. As the battle raged on, Williams sent the squadron's gunships into the fight.

Our 12 or so gunships, including mine, were to form up into a daisy chain, a large circle of gunships with massed firepower to attack a target. Our chase ship, manned by my buddies SP4 George Gavaria and Sergeant Bruce DeHart, would join us. We began to fly around the mountain at about 500 feet. The weather was good with clear skies, ideal for flying and shooting. We began our assault on the mountain as the sun began to set.

As our pilots climbed into the chain, a gunship above us dropped down towards our position and almost struck our main rotor blades. Our pilot dropped collective and we fell about a hundred feet before regaining control. *That was a very close call.* Carefully, he flew back up and entered the chain in another slot. We were engaging in a very dangerous game of aerial ballet.

We began to take fire from heavy machine guns on the side of the mountain. .51mm cal tracers arced up at our daisy chain as their gunners tried to shoot us out of the sky. My stomach tightened with every round as those long fingers of death flickered past us.

★ ★ ★

On the mountaintop, SP4 William "Doc" Byrd, a medic with the Troop C Blues, was busy treating the wounded of the 3rd and 4th Squads on the left flank of the anthill. He thought back on this incident in particular:

> A sniper shot my buddy Andy Lowery in the pelvis and then another round hit his shirt pocket, setting his mail letters on fire. I quickly treated Lowery and also a very badly wounded trooper from Delta Troop who was nearby.

After that, Doc did something crazy. He pulled out his pistol and began shooting at the area where the sniper had been firing from. Another rifleman, Carl Hudelson, came over to help with the wounded. As they treated the wounded men, they took turns throwing hand grenades up the hill. The enemy threw them back, and one exploded next to Doc and Hudelson. Hudelson threw himself on top of Doc to shield him from the blast. The grenade sent shrapnel between his eyes and forehead, causing Hudelson to become one of the wounded Doc was now treating.

Also on the left flank was Sergeant Medina's 4th Squad. Medina began throwing hand grenades up the hill as he moved his squad into the tall elephant grass to look for snipers. One of his men, PFC Peter Burbank, got lost in the tall grass. He described how:

> I couldn't see anything and lost contact with my squad. I found a trail on the side of the hill and moved along it until I came upon a dead man from Delta Troop. Just then, a sniper opened fire on me, and I hit the ground and tried to take off my web belt because it had a bunch of grenades and a claymore mine on it. An enemy round hit my M-16 magazine and set it on fire. I grabbed some grenades, threw them at the sniper and then fired some rounds at him. Somehow, I managed to find my way back to my squad without getting shot.

By now, Captain Knowlen had recognized that this was a one-sided fight with the enemy well-fortified inside their bunkers and spider holes on the hill. He called Major Williams on the radio.

"Sir, we are taking deadly fire from these bunkers."

"Copy that. Make a sweep of the area, collect your wounded, and pull back up the ridge. I'm sending the gunships in."

★ ★ ★

About ten minutes later, we got a call from Major Williams ordering the gunships to assault the Crow's Foot. The long daisy chain formation dropped altitude and commenced its attack. We followed the ships ahead of us, watching how they dove down towards the hilltop and fired their rockets and machine guns at the enemy positions. Suddenly, from a tree-covered ridgeline, a 12.7mm heavy antiaircraft machine gun opened fire at us.

This was no ordinary enemy bunker complex. This was a major NVA regimental headquarters with fixed antiaircraft heavy machine guns. Intelligence later identified this position as the 18th NVA Regiment.

Tracer fire came towards us, flying under and over our aircraft. It was the scariest thing I saw during my time in Vietnam. Finally, our turn came to dive on the target. As we rolled in, our pilots opened fire with a barrage of 2.75-inch-high explosive rockets. Enemy snipers and machine gunners fired up at us from the elephant grass. As we flew over them, we sprayed them with our M-60 door guns. Sergeant Jim Barrett, a door gunner of Troop C, told of how:

> We made our run and began firing at the bunkers when all of a sudden, we heard a loud, popping noise, and a big round crashed through our chin bubble on the nose of our bird. It was an NVA .51 cal heavy machine gun that hit us. My pilot, CWO Frank Moser, slumped forward and we thought he was hit, but he raised his head and yelled out, "Them dirty sons of bitches!" As bad as the situation was, we all started laughing. When we rolled in again, they kept shooting at us. Later we were told the NVA gunners were chained to their guns.

One of our lead gunships, flown by Major Dick Marshall with SP4 Don Coshey as crew chief, got hit by the antiaircraft fire coming out of a rocket run. SP4 Coshey remembered this as follows:

> We took some .51 cal rounds through the floor which knocked out our center and upper control panels. We did not know the extent of our damage until we started our attack run and the machine guns and rockets would not fire. So, we ended up having to use our door guns to protect us from enemy fire.

As dusk descended over the mountain, Major Williams ordered the gunships to return to LZ DOG. We refueled and loaded up the rocket pods, then stood by waiting to be called back into action. The aero rifle lift platoon flew in some fresh troops and ammunition and evacuated the dead and wounded. LTC Shoemaker flew out to the mountain LZ to check on the situation. He conferred with Captain Knowlen to get an up-to-date picture of the action. The Blues set up a defense perimeter, installed claymore mines and trip wires, and dug in for the night.

A light drizzle of rain began to fall, making for a cold, wet, miserable, and sleepless night for the battle-weary infantrymen. The enemy had withdrawn from the hilltop bunkers, taking up positions on the sides of the mountain. Later that night, the enemy sent probes up the mountain to test the defense perimeter. The Blues riflemen rolled hand grenades down the sides of the ridgeline to keep the NVA at bay. All night long, flares were fired to illuminate the darkness. A battery of Division Artillery 155mm cannons, code-named "Sticky Cider 63," were on tap for support missions. Just after darkness set in, they bracketed the lower side of the mountain with protective fires. PFC Burbank recounted:

> I remember seeing a long line of lanterns winding down to the bottom of the mountain and leading over towards a village in the valley. This was the enemy, collecting its dead and wounded from the mountain.

When dawn broke, the Blues made a sweep of the ridge to collect their dead and wounded. They found some enemy weapons but no enemy dead. The final score for the battle was three Americans KIA and about thirty WIA. Enemy KIA was unknown as they had been evacuated overnight. The battle showed that the enemy was well established in the Kim Son Valley. Intelligence determined that the Crow's Foot was a part of the NVA's regimental defense complex, which was set up to protect their headquarters deeper into the valley.

On February 15, two days after the 9th Cavalry recon operation, the 2nd Brigade deployed its 1/5th, 2/5th, and 2/12th Infantry Battalions into the Crow's Foot to root out the NVA regiment. It was a bloody campaign. It took days of artillery strikes and a B–52 Arc Light raid to knock out the enemy from their bunkers. This battle resulted in 312 NVA dead and 23 Americans KIA. The 1st of the 9th had once again found the enemy for the 1st Cavalry Division.

CHAPTER TWELVE

Aero Scout White Platoon

Mike

We returned to base camp at An Khe on March 6. Operation *Masher-White Wing* was considered a military success by division headquarters. They published a newsletter and distributed it to all the units of the 1st Cavalry. We were informed that we had engaged three hardcore regiments of the 3rd Yellow (Sao Vang) Division in Bong Son: the 2nd Viet Cong Main Force Regiment, the 18th Regiment, and the 22nd NVA Regiment. In a 42-day campaign, we killed over 1,300 of the enemy forces. We lost 288 Americans killed in action and 990 wounded. We captured and destroyed tons of enemy supplies and equipment. Our allies—made up of elements of the 1st Marine Division, the ARVN 22nd Infantry Division, and the Republic of Korea (ROK) Army units—accounted for more than 800 enemy dead.

None of this meant anything to us. We were all just glad to be alive and back at our base camp for some much-needed rest. We spent the days refitting our equipment, drawing new supplies, and pulling a lot of overdue repairs on our aircraft and weapons.

I was totally exhausted from the constant pace of flight operations and had lost 10 pounds due to the stress. When I got a chance to go to Japan for some R&R, I jumped at it. I got my orders and put on my summer khaki uniform before heading to the airfield to catch an Air Force transport plane to Saigon.

The 1st Cavalry had been given permission to wear our combat boots bloused like the paratroopers, which gave us a little status. After the grueling weeks in combat, it was good to feel a little special.

I flew down to Saigon on a C-130 transport where I boarded a civilian contracted 707 jetliner heading stateside with returning troops. I got dropped off at Kadena Air Force Base in Okinawa for a connecting flight to Japan. I wished I could be going home with the other men on the 707, but it wasn't my time yet.

I never made it to Japan and ended up spending my whole leave on Okinawa. It was a good, relaxing vacation. When it was over, I did not want to go back to Vietnam. I did not want to go back to the nightmare.

On the way back to Vietnam, I ran into some transportation problems. I spent a few days stranded at the Air Force 9th Aerial Port at Tan Son Nhut Air Base. Every time I was placed on a flight roster, I got bumped off by a higher-ranking military passenger. On top of that, they were shipping new troops out to their units on the C-130 transports and they had priority over anyone on leave.

I had to put up overnight in hotels. In one hotel, there was a bar on the top floor where you could sit and drink a beer at night while firefights raged off in the distance. It was a strange experience.

Compared to my time in the jungle, life in Saigon looked good to me. When the soldiers there found out I was with the 1st Cavalry, they bought me drinks. I got a lot of free drinks there. Those boys had no idea how difficult it was to be a trooper out in the boondocks of the Central Highlands.

On my last day at Tan Son Nhut, one of my pilots got off one of the landing planes for his own R&R.

"Kelley! What are you doing here! You okay? The first sergeant listed you as AWOL!"

"Not AWOL. Not me. I've been stranded here in Saigon waiting for a plane to take me back. I'm a lower priority over here right now." I gestured towards all the soldiers waiting for planes. His eyes got big as he looked at how many people were waiting.

"I get it. Wow. I'll vouch for you when I get back. Tell the first sergeant you spoke to me and I said it was okay for you to be delayed, that it wasn't your fault. Good luck!"

I finally got aboard a C-130 that day, but my adventures in getting back to base camp were not over. We headed north, but the plane could not land at An Khe due to bad weather. I got dropped off about 50 miles away at the Qhi Nhon Air Force Base. I spent the night there and the next day managed to hitch a ride with some 1st Cavalry troopers who were heading back in their Dodge ¾ ton cargo truck. I got to ride on the back of the dusty truck, in the hot sun. I was starting to feel like I was back in hell again.

About halfway to An Khe we ran out of gas and got a flat. Luckily, we were near a Republic of Korea base camp on Highway 19. As we pulled in to see if they could help us, we were greeted by a Korean officer who quickly ordered his men to fix our flat and give us some gas. They also gave us a cold drink as they worked on the truck. It was a welcome treat and felt so good going down my dry and dusty throat. It didn't take them long to finish, and we loaded back into the truck to continue our journey to base camp.

The Korean officer told us "Good luck!" and waved at us as we departed the camp.

By the time I got dropped off at the main road for the 9th Cavalry, I was covered with a film of road dirt and my uniform was soaked with sweat. I was a sorry-looking soldier as I walked up the road and reported to the Troop C orderly room. The first sergeant stormed out of his office.

"Kelley! You finally came back, huh? We don't put up with soldiers going AWOL around here, you hear?"

"Top Sergeant, I didn't go AWOL. I got stuck in…"

"I don't want to hear it! No excuses!"

"I saw my pilot in Saigon. He said he can vouch for me."

"Sure, Kelley. Nice one. Get into your duty uniform and report to your platoon sergeant. I don't want any more trouble from you."

Unknown to me, my old platoon sergeant had been sent away for medical treatment while I was on R&R and we now had a new platoon sergeant. I reported to him quickly after my arrival.

"You're the piece of crap who went AWOL on us, huh? What kind of a soldier are you? A piss poor one, I'm sure. No good little Gold Bricker over here, leaving while the rest of us are here doing our duty."

Gold Bricker is Army slang for lazy goof off. I did not appreciate being called that, or any of the other names he called me. It wasn't my fault that I had been stranded in Saigon. He was just being a hard ass. Had he even looked at my good performance record? *What can he do to me anyway? I'm already here in Vietnam, it can't get any worse than this.*

"Go to hell!" I was mad. I should have known better, but I couldn't help it. The platoon sergeant was a lifer, a career man, and I was just a young trooper.

"Go to hell, huh? Sure. You are out of the weapons platoon as of right now. I'm sending you to the Scout platoon, Kelley. You belong with those misfits!"

It was known that Scout platoon enjoyed flying at treetop level in their little OH-13S observation helicopters, and that they took a lot of ground fire on their low-level recon missions. They got into places a gunship could not go. *I guess he* can *do something to me.* I collected my gear and went over to the Scout platoon to report to SP6 Russell, my new platoon sergeant.

Russell welcomed me and assigned me to aircraft number 63-9156, an OH-13 S. I liked that bird and knew it well, as I had trained on it at Fort Rucker's aviation school.

It wasn't long before I made some new friends in the Scouts. PFC Richard Denning and SP5 Craig Kasel were especially helpful and friendly to me. As it turned out, I liked my new home.

My first mission with the Scouts was Operation *Lincoln.*

By this time, I had been awarded the Air Medal with three oak leaf clusters for all of my combat assault missions with the gunships, and had almost enough time logged for a fourth oak leaf. I would log many more missions with the Scout platoon.

On March 25 we moved out of An Khe and headed west to the Pleiku Province along the Cambodian border. We arrived at the Oasis, a large landing zone out near the Ia Drang Valley, southwest of the city of Pleiku. This would be our forward base for Operation *Lincoln.*

Our enemy in this area was the 32nd NVA Regiment, the 33rd NVA Regiment, and the 66th NVA Regiment. They had large base camps on and around the Chu Pong mountain close to the Cambodian border. They also had base camps across the border in the Ho Chi Minh Trail complex.

The 9th Cavalry was tasked with going out into the vast jungle wilderness to find enemy forces. The Scouts played an important part in this operation. The Ia Drang River flowed across the Cambodian border east to west and then had tributaries that ran northward. These were good areas to scout for enemy movements where NVA patrols crossed the rivers. One day we were out on recon, flying out over the thick jungle north of the Chu Pong mountain. We flew over the river, crisscrossing its banks at low-level, looking for signs of enemy footpaths and trails. We were at treetop level, so they could not see us until we were on top of them.

As we began to cross over the riverbank, we looked down and saw about a dozen NVA on the bank of the river. They appeared to be bathing and collecting drinking water. I dropped a smoke marker and then my pilot made a tight turn to make another pass over them. As the smoke billowed up from the riverbank, the NVA ran under the trees for cover. We called the gunships who were flying about a half mile behind us and told them what we had found. They quickly came in and made a run on the NVA under the trees. Rockets and machine guns fired rapidly before they flew up and turned around for a second pass.

The area was so wild and thickly wooded that there was no way we could have inserted a Blues platoon for a ground search. We marked our map with the coordinates for squadron HQ. Then we returned to LZ Oasis, where I refueled my ship and inspected it for battle damage. Once I had it ready to fly for the next day's missions, I returned to my tent and cleaned up with a field bath.

Taking a bath with soap and water from your steel helmet was considered a luxury out there in the boondocks. We always had a good supply of water from a large water trailer we called a water buffalo that parked next to the mess tent. I bathed and shaved, and then reused the bath water to wash my clothes after. We always hung our wet clothes on the ropes that held up our tents, and they dried pretty fast in the heat of the afternoon.

After getting cleaned up, it was almost time for the evening meal, the highlight of my day. We usually got a hot breakfast and a hot dinner, and lunch was a box of C-rations. C-rations were assorted canned meals, like hot dogs and beans, that we usually ate cold and straight out of the can.

The troops lined up at the mess tent at around 1800 hours every day. Sometimes a medic waited at the front of the line to give us a malaria pill or some other form of medicine that we were required to take. On occasion, we were given a pack of cigarettes or a candy bar. The enlisted men brought their mess kits to eat out of, while the officers got to eat off of plates that were kept in a special wooden box.

The cooks always did their best to create a good meal for us with their limited supplies. We didn't get much fresh food, most of what we ate came from tin cans. Large "Number 10" cans held pre-cooked meats like turkey and ham. Vegetables came in smaller cans. Potatoes were made from a flaky mix, and the eggs came in a powder form and were almost always served scrambled when cooked. The bacon was like rubber. Usually, sliced bread was offered with each meal, but occasionally the cooks would make hot biscuits. For dessert we got some type of canned fruit. When we were in the field, the cooks prepared our meals using portable stoves. They worked hard to prepare our meals, especially with the difficulties presented by combat conditions. They tried to satisfy everyone as much as possible.

I remember one cook named Scotty. Scotty was a short, muscular Black sergeant who used to whip up a batch of homemade honey dip donuts almost every month as a special treat for "his boys." He was a really nice guy. Once, I came down with a fever and dysentery and was restricted to my cot for days. Scotty came by regularly during that time to check on me. He brought me "fresh" fruit that had come through the supply system.

"You need to get something in you, Kelley, you don't want to get dehydrated."

Scotty was like a friendly uncle, and he really enjoyed looking after us young, homesick soldiers.

After we ate our meals, we washed our mess kits in large, metal barrels full of hot water. The water was heated to a prescribed temperature by a submerged mini-heater that was intended to prevent outbreaks of dysentery. We had to wash our mess kits in two barrels of hot, soapy water and rinse them in two barrels of hot clear water.

As we finished, the mail clerk showed up. If you were lucky, you would get a letter from home. Some guys looked forward to mail more than chow. If you got a goodie box it was an occasion, and all your buddies would wait for you to open it up so they could help you eat the contents. If you got a box of homemade cookies, you'd be lucky to eat a few before they were gone.

One of our Blues was an Italian kid from New York who got a box of Italian treats from his father every month.

"Kelley? You want a slice?" He would ask as he sliced off a piece of salami with his bayonet. The experience of eating homemade salami near the Cambodian border is one thing I will never forget.

In the field, we each got a warm can of beer and a warm can of soda every night. Some guys swapped beers for sodas with each other. Each platoon also got an SP Pack with goodies every month. We quickly swarmed the box to snag the best goodies; cigarettes, cigars, chewing tobacco, writing paper, chewing gum, candy bars. Everything a guy stuck in the boondocks could enjoy. The crewmen who were on the last flights of the day would return to the leftovers, like Pall Malls or Chesterfield cigarettes. All the good stuff would be gone by then.

When we returned to our "pup" tents, we would write a letter home using a candle or a flashlight. Then we would sit around and talk about the day or tell stories of our lives before the Army. Usually, these stories were about old girlfriends or cars. I always found these stories fascinating, because the men came from all over the United States and had grown up in all sorts of areas, from small towns to big cities. I learned so much about places that I had previously only seen on a map. I got an education from the Army that I wasn't expecting, learning about people in a way I couldn't have done otherwise. It made me into the person I turned out to be and I was grateful for those experiences. The recruiter never talked about that aspect of becoming an Army soldier and for me, it was an added bonus.

Sometimes field duty involved pulling guard duty on the outer defense perimeter. On one of the first evenings that I remember doing this with my platoon, we were assigned a sector to guard and told to report to a 25th Infantry Division M-113 armored personnel carrier (APC). We were greeted by a lieutenant who briefed us on what he expected of us before taking us to a couple of foxholes about a dozen feet from the barbed wire of the outer perimeter.

"Get in and keep your eyes open!"

We got in.

It got dark. *I can't even see my hand in front of my face. How am I supposed to know if the enemy is coming?* We sat there, listening to the sounds of the jungle while talking in whispers to each other. We took turns sitting in the bottom of the hole to smoke a cigarette.

At about 0300 hours, it suddenly got quiet. All the jungle noises just stopped. We got nervous and readied our weapons to fire. We were not infantrymen who knew the jungle like it was their backyard. After a long, tense wait, we decided we should check in with the lieutenant. I was the one who was voted in to be the man to go back up the hill and find him.

I slowly crept toward the APC and when I got to the top of the hill, I could just make out the silhouette of the M-113. I made my way around to the rear of the vehicle and knocked on the hatch. It opened up to reveal the inside, which was lit by a dim, red lamp. The group of soldiers inside were busy playing cards. A cloud of cigarette smoke poured out as I leaned inside to talk.

"What the hell are you doing up here, soldier!?" To say the lieutenant was upset by my presence would be an understatement.

"Sir, we think there is something going on down near the foxhole. The jungle just got quiet and we are worried."

"Goddammit soldier, there is nothing going on down there! You could have gotten shot coming up that hill in the dark! Get your ass back down to the foxhole. If anything happens, you will hear our guns and know! Now Get!"

As I turned to leave, I looked atop the APC and saw the outline of a soldier standing behind an M-2 .50 cal heavy machine gun. It was good to know we had someone looking over us. I slowly found my way back to the foxhole and rejoined my nervous buddies. We shivered in that foxhole all night, and when dawn came, we were happy to see the lieutenant arrive to relieve us from duty. It had been a long and sleepless night.

At dawn, a pair of Scouts were taking off to patrol the perimeter. Their Lycoming, turbo-charged six-cylinder engines made a loud roar as they came to life and began to warm up, their rotor blades spinning faster with each rotation of the engine. As we made our way to the mess tent for a hot breakfast, the Scouts lifted off and flew out to begin their morning mission. Their rotor blades beat the misty air above the LZ.

Pancakes, maple syrup, and a hot cup of coffee tasted so good after our long night on the perimeter. We wolfed down our meal and returned to our tents to pick up our toolbox and report for our day's work repairing the helicopters. My ship needed a new hydraulic servo for the flight controls. The long hours of flying and the harsh, grimy conditions we encountered in the boondocks in Vietnam wore out the hydraulics a lot faster than the easy and clean conditions of stateside duty.

Action in the Ia Drang–Chu Pong area was sporadic as the NVA had taken to the ground, trying to avoid contact. They only came out to fight when they had the advantage, such as when poor weather prevented us from supporting our infantry out on patrols, or if they saw they outnumbered us and had an opportunity to ambush our patrols. The NVA were good jungle fighters, and experts with small unit tactics.

A typical NVA fighter was about 22 years old, stood at about five feet, four inches tall, and weighed about 115 pounds. He may have grown up on a farm or small village and was probably drafted for service. He was highly motivated and disciplined. His leaders were well-trained officers and non-commissioned officers. Each unit had a pesky communist political officer who made sure they all believed strongly in their government's policies of National Liberation.

An NVA soldier could improvise and adapt to almost any situation. He lived under harsh conditions, subsisting mainly on a diet of rice with an occasional piece of chicken, fish, duck, or hot peppers. His diet was supplemented by wild game caught while he was on his patrols. Despite being afflicted with malaria and other tropical diseases, he fought the "dau tranh" (the struggle) against his enemies. Unlike American forces, the NVA were cut off from their families and homes, with little or no communication. If they were lucky, they received a few letters a year. On average, they served about three years of combat before being killed, wounded, or evacuated for serious illness. Their lives were difficult with little reward. They had no DEROS.

U.S. Forces could rotate home after a year in the war zone, while the NVA stayed on in the jungle to fight. The three NVA regiments in the Chu Pong–Ia Drang area were first rate troops. Most of them fought to the death. Some were brutal, and it was known that they would torture American prisoners. In the November 1965 battle of Ia Drang Valley, the NVA shot down a Troop C gunship which crashed in the jungle. We learned that the NVA slowly executed the survivors. One of my greatest fears was being shot down and captured by the NVA. It was a fate far worse than instant death.

On March 30, the 1st of the 9th Cavalry made contact with a large NVA force west of the Chu Pong mountain along the Cambodian border. Bravo Troop Scouts had spotted 32 NVA in a wooded area. The Alpha Troop Blues were inserted to conduct a ground recon patrol and found the area was heavily fortified with a bunker complex. As they swept through the area, the lone patrol was ambushed by a superior force. CWO Dave Bray recalled how:

> The Blues landed in the middle of an NVA regiment and the platoon took heavy casualties from the fierce machine gun and automatic weapons fire. The aero rifle lift platoon was called in to extract the Blues and came under withering enemy crossfire. Four pilots were killed, and two helicopters were shot down. Nineteen of the Blues were killed. On one of the Slicks, both pilots were shot up and the crew chief, SP4 McKee, had to pull the co-pilot from his seat and take over the flight controls. Despite having no flight experience, he was able to fly the stricken ship back to the special force's airstrip at Plei Mei and land it. The squadron commander, LTC Robert M. Shoemaker, pinned a Distinguished Flying Cross on him before he promptly got on another helicopter and flew back into action. His aircraft had 29 bullet holes in the pilot's cockpit. Eventually, the 1/12th Cavalry Battalion arrived at the battle to take over the contact.

The next day, CWO Bray returned to the area and spotted over 100 NVA. He and his observer-door gunner dropped CS and smoke canisters on the target and called in a strike by the Air Rocket Artillery (ARA), who fired salvos of 2.75-inch rockets on the NVA force. Bray then called the Air Force at Pleiku Air Base. Baron 1-9 deployed a flight of F-4 Phantoms who dropped napalm on the NVA.

A few days later, Bray spotted another bunch of NVA under the trees in a chow line near the Cambodian border. Once again, he and his observer-door gunner dropped CS and smoke canisters on the enemy. His door gunner fired his M-16 at them as Bray fired off a salvo of 2.75-inch rockets. He then got on the radio and called in an artillery strike. After the artillery had worked over the area, the 1/12th Cavalry Battalion arrived on station and made contact with the NVA. When the battle ended, the total enemy body count was 197. By the time Operation Lincoln ended on April 8, the total enemy body count was 453, most of them killed from devastating artillery fire. As the old saying goes, "Payback is a bitch."

We packed up our equipment and tents and pulled out of LZ Oasis to return to our base camp at An Khe. Back at base, we caught up with making repairs to our OH-13S helicopters and pulling routine inspections. The officers had completed their hootches up on the hillside in officer's country by this time. Some even had front porches that they could sit on at night and relax after a hard day of flying missions.

The enlisted men began buying materials from the village of An Khe to start construction on their own hootches. They mixed and poured cement floors, built the framework, put up some side boards, and added a sheet-metal roof. Large open windows with screens allowed for a breeze at night. Each hootch had about eight rooms that held two men each. They built five of these hootches and moved out of the old, worn, mildewed tents and into their new quarters.

Then post engineers came by when we were in the field and built a nice wooden mess hall and a new orderly room. We no longer lived in the tent city.

The first sergeant always had plenty of work details to keep us busy. We had to pull KP duty in the mess hall, dig grease traps, clean the metal barrels that held the water for rinsing, haul trash to the dump, and clean and repair the latrines. We all dreaded getting called to do the worst job of all: to burn shit.

Shit detail was a dirty, smelly job. The latrine was an open-air wooden shack with six toilet seat openings. Under the enclosed seats behind the latrine was an opening where 55-gallon drums had been cut down and inserted under the toilet seats. They had to be pulled out every so often and the barrels of waste had to be burned. We would add diesel fuel and gasoline to the waste pile and set it all on fire. It had to be stirred and have fuel added to it every few minutes to keep it burning hot, and a huge black cloud of smoke would billow into the air. The only good thing about this detail was that you got to read a bunch of *Playboy* magazines that the guys brought to the fire to pass the time.

When you finished shit detail, the first thing you'd do was go back to the hootch, strip off your clothes, and head for the shower. The guys built a field shower, a platform made out of an old wooden pallet with a 55-gallon drum on top. It was rigged with a showerhead and a valve that would open and close the water flow. To take a shower, you lugged a five-gallon can of water to the drum and poured it in. Then you stood under the showerhead, pulled the valve, and stood under the onslaught of cold water that poured out. Even though the water was cold, it always felt good to get a shower.

After our shower, we put on a clean set of clothes and washed our dirty ones in a bucket of water the next day. The harsh Army soap we were given to wash our clothes with eventually wore out the fabric, and we began to have holes in our pants. We were given three work uniforms and our supply room had issued us one set of jungle fatigues. Once our underwear wore out, we had to go without it because no underwear was available in the system. Some items of clothing that we could not obtain from supply were available down in the village on the black market. Vietnamese workers would steal these items from the warehouses and sell them to us.

When we returned from the field, we were given a lot of mail that had been held up in the Army's postal system. I received a box full of Christmas gifts that included a homemade fruitcake from my mother. It was packed with popcorn to protect the contents. My buddies not only ate the very stale fruitcake, but they ate the three-month-old popcorn too! My sister had sent me an electric razor that I couldn't use because we had no electricity.

One of the best items in my mail was a package from an elementary school teacher in Arlington, a city west of Boston. A girlfriend of mine had a little brother in the fifth grade there and he asked his teacher to have the class send me some greeting cards. They all drew pictures with some words of support to the troops. One card had a picture of a soldier pushing a lawn mower that was cutting down Viet Cong soldiers with the words "Mow Them Down G.I." written in childlike crayon letters. My buddies and I really enjoyed looking at those cards. They were a big morale booster.

One of the best parts about being back at An Khe was the chance to go down to the village on a day pass. The village was made up of a mixture of cement buildings and tin-roofed shacks alongside of Highway 19. There were a lot of little bars, storefronts, some restaurants, open markets, a barbershop, and a photoshop (which lost my photos). There was also a government-monitored area called Sin City, which consisted of a series of bars that catered to lonesome G.I.s. One day an ARVN soldier threw a hand grenade into one of these bars, wounding a bunch of American soldiers. The military police came in and made all the Americans leave the area.

We were not liked by the Vietnamese troops. They considered us to be overpaid, overfed, and oversexed. As their allies, the American troops felt they were unreliable and just wanted us to fight the war for them. They had poor morale due to the corruption in their Army and Saigon.

For the next month, we flew recon missions around base camp, providing security for road convoys and base security patrols. One day, we flew about twenty miles north of An Khe to a place called LZ 9. There was a small operation going on in that area and my pilot landed in the LZ to confer with the infantry commander. He left the engine running and the rotor turning as I sat in the observer gunner door position.

Suddenly, a Viet Cong sniper opened up from the jungle north of us. My pilot ran back to the ship and we quickly took off. We flew a low-level pattern over the trees, trying to spot the sniper. The troops on the LZ perimeter opened fire towards the area where the sniper fire had come from. After a fifteen-minute search, we had not found the sniper and he had stopped firing. We called it a day and returned to base.

A few days later, my buddy PFC Richard Denning was flying with CWO Jerry Grimm along the Song Ba River, south of An Khe. They were on a first light security patrol when they came under heavy small arms fire. A round hit the engine and they lost power, forced to make an emergency landing in the middle of the river. Luckily it was shallow when they set down and they evacuated the ship and made their way to the opposite bank of the river. They had called a Mayday emergency to the command post to let them know they had been shot down. They took up a defense position as they waited for help to arrive.

About 15 minutes later, a pair of gunships showed up with a single UH-1D maintenance bird. The squadron maintenance officer arrived with three maintenance technicians to inspect the downed helicopter for damage. It was determined that the ship was not flyable and would have to be evacuated. They called in for a heavy lift CH-47 Chinook from the 228th Assault Helicopter Battalion to come and pick up the damaged bird.

After the ship was lifted out by the CH-47, the Scout crew climbed aboard the UH-1D with the maintenance crew and took off for base camp, where the OH-13 was delivered to the 15th Maintenance Battalion for repairs.

In May, we got a new squadron commander as LTC Robert M. Shoemaker rotated out and LTC James C. Smith took over command of the 1st Squadron, 9th Cavalry. Smith carried on the Air Cavalry traditions like his predecessors, all schooled in the art of air mobility operations. LTC Smith sent Troop C on its next big mission, Operation *Hawthorne*.

We were deployed up to Dak To, a desolate special forces camp in a valley surrounded by a chain of rugged mountains not far from the Cambodian border. We set up our forward camp in a large field near the airstrip.

I was immediately placed on KP duty, I didn't even get a chance to set up my tent shelter first. I had to help put up the mess tent, set up the stoves and cooking equipment, unload supplies, and help dig a large trash pit behind the mess tent. It was a hard, dirty job.

As we dug the six-foot-deep pit, one of the soldiers decided he wasn't going to dig anymore dirt. He lit up a cigarette and leaned on his shovel, watching the rest of us work. Just then, the mess sergeant came along and saw him goofing off.

"Get back to digging, soldier!"

He took his shovel and put a small amount of dirt on it before looking back up at the sergeant.

"Sarge, you can work me long, but you can't work me hard."

The sergeant got mad and walked away. What could he do? Send him to Vietnam? The soldier stood in the hole laughing.

"I guess I pissed the old sarge off, hey guys?"

By the time I got off KP duty it was dark. I fumbled with the ropes and stake of my tent, trying to set it up. I was filthy, sweaty, and very tired. I did the best I could to secure the tent and then I rolled into my sleeping bag. Sleep came quickly that night. A few hours later, a strong, windy storm blew over the camp and took my shelter away. I was left lying in my sleeping bag out in the wide open under the rain. I was so disgusted and tired that I just pulled my bag over my head and went back to sleep.

At dawn, I woke up soaking wet. My sleeping bag was like a large green sponge that was full of water. A hot cup of Army coffee brought me back to life and I went off in search of my shelter half "pup" tent. The Scouts and the gunships went out with the Blues to recon and screen the mountains and jungle west of Dak To for signs of enemy forces near the Cambodian border. This area was known as "Indian Country" and was very dangerous, as it was close to well defended enemy base camps of the NVA B-3 Front.

Fighting in the jungle and the mountains was a challenge for our troops. When you fight in the jungle, you feel isolated from the outside world. The strange noises and sounds, the constant dampness and oppressive heat—the burden of carrying backpacks, extra ammo, C-rations, web gear, extra water canteens, hand grenades, radio sets, and machine guns—and the ever-present, blood-sucking leeches that got inside your nose, ears, and penis, were all a constant menace. Add to that the threat from poisonous spiders, malaria-carrying mosquitos, and viper snakes who could paralyze or kill you with one venomous bite.

The weary, sleepless troops fighting in the dark jungle went through a hellish experience that most people can't even imagine. They had the toughest job in the Army. To advance on enemy positions, they had to walk or crawl forward on slippery, muddy hills and mountains, sometimes losing their footing and falling back down the hill into rocks, trees, or bamboo thickets. Getting wounded meant they were exposed to the millions of microorganisms that thrived in the putrid jungle, and many men got major infections. Their filthy, sweaty bodies were breeding grounds for bacterial infections. Parasites would enter their bodies and live for months or years inside their warm bloodstreams. Waiting for a medical evacuation could take hours or days, depending on the weather and circumstances. Some medical evacuation helicopters were shot down by enemy fire and never arrived. Men often died from loss of blood, shock, or wounds that they could have survived if they had received proper treatment in time.

Jungle fighting wasn't just hard for the American troops, though. The North Vietnamese struggled as well. Other than the men who actually fought in the jungle, no one really knows what it was like. Movies and books have tried to portray it, but those brave men actually lived it.

In any army, the infantryman is at the tip of the combat spear. It takes 10 support troops to keep one infantryman in the field. Of the 280,000 troops in Vietnam in 1966, only about a third of them were infantrymen, who were the ones doing the bulk of the fighting. This is not to say that the armored troops, artillerymen, or even helicopter crewmen did not see plenty of action: they did. But fighting the enemy on foot, humping 70 or more pounds of gear up mountains, and engaging in hand-to-hand fighting was different from any of the other combat experiences. Support troops did fight off enemy ambushes, but they did not slog in the jungles.

Winston Churchill once noted, "The front is a very small club!" He was referencing the fighting in World War I but it is a relevant comment in regard to any war. The infantry did the most amount of fighting with the least amount of men. In some cases, infantry companies were understrength, with some platoons having only 25 or 30 men. Wounded and sick depleted a platoon after a battle and bringing in cherries or NFGs downgraded a unit's effectiveness. It took time to train the new guys.

I learned to have a healthy respect for our Blues platoon in Troop C. For the most part, they kept to themselves and didn't mingle with the other platoons. I was fortunate to have befriended PFC Peter Burbank of our Blues platoon.

Peter was from the Boston area, like me, and we hit it off great. Through him, I met many of the Blues and often was invited to their tent to hang out. It was a great privilege to be in the presence of the warriors who wore the Combat Infantry Badge.

In Troop C, the Blues were elite troopers. They were so proud of the CIB, that many would choose their CIB over a Bronze Star if given the choice. I saw guys give up easy jobs to transfer to the Blues to earn a CIB in combat. It was a badge that stood for honor and courage.

Upon completion of our missions at Dak To, we packed up and moved to Kontum to set up our forward base near a Special Forces camp. The Special Forces allowed us to use their small post exchange (PX). I bought some soap and a Japanese 35mm camera. I loaded it with color slide film to begin taking pictures. My first picture was of a beautiful sunset over the mountains. One of my Scout NCOs knew all about 35mm cameras and taught me how to use it.

I had a lot of opportunities to take some great pictures while I was out on recon patrols. It was rough, rugged country where it wasn't uncommon to see deer, wild pigs, peacocks, and the occasional elephant or tiger. There was a spectacular waterfall in the middle of nowhere that caught my eye as well. Back in the early 1900s, the area had been favored by big game hunters like Teddy Roosevelt.

One day, one of our Scouts shot a deer and an aero rifle lift platoon Slick flew out to pick it up and bring it back to camp. Some of the men were experienced hunters and they cleaned it out and cut it up into steaks for the cooks to grill. I had a small piece, but I did not like it much. It tasted very sweet. The outdoor country boys ate it up though. I guess I was too much of a soft city slicker.

While at Kontum, we flew security patrols around the camp perimeter and recon patrols out along the Cambodian border west of Kontum. A few miles across the border was the famous Ho Chi Minh Trail, where the NVA brought fresh troops and supplies down from the north. The

Chu Pong mountain area was their command-and-control point, and small base camps were located across the border as way stations where the troopers could rest and train in preparation for combat. We knew they were there, but we were not allowed to cross the border and attack these camps. White House orders. Go figure. Politicians running the military machine.

On many occasions when the 1st Cavalry managed to dominate battle, the NVA would withdraw across the border into their Cambodian sanctuaries to avoid our air assaults.

There was a famous incident where a Troop C gunship was chasing some NVA who fled over the border near a Cambodian border patrol post that had a flagpole with a Cambodian flag flying in the breeze. When the gunship straddled the border post, the Cambodian guards opened fire on our aircraft. This pissed off the pilots, who then ordered the door gunners to return fire, which they did. The Cambodians ran off into the jungle to hide. The gunship then hovered over the flagpole and the door gunner got out onto the skids and tore the flag off of the pole. That flag was hung in a place of honor in the Officers' Club back at An Khe Base Camp.

By mid-June, we had completed several recon missions west of Kontum, including the insertion of the Blues on the ground to check out possible enemy activity, but we didn't find anything in the area. The NVA were holding out across the border, waiting for us to move out. On June 19, we received orders to pack up and relocate to a new area of operations.

Troop C was sent down south along the coastline, to a place called Tuy Hoa, to take part in a new operation called *Nathan Hale*. We set up our new base camp on the white sandy beach next to the beautiful bluish-green South China Sea. It was the kind of place where someone would go on a tropical vacation in peacetime. It was not, however, a good place to operate aircraft and vehicles. The fine, gritty sand damaged engines and quickly wore out parts.

CHAPTER THIRTEEN

Charlie Alpha Combat Assault

Pete

Two recon platoons, one from the 1st Battalion, 8th Cavalry, and our own Troop C Blues, air assaulted into two small landing zones in the mountains west of Tuy Hoa. A wide oxcart trail led up a hill into heavy woods on the side and the top.

Our aero rifle lift platoon of UH–1D Huey Slicks air assaulted us into a small LZ at the bottom of the hill. The 1/8th Recon Platoon was air assaulted up to a small LZ closer to the hill by the 229th Assault Helicopter Battalion.

As we moved out on our recon patrol, we spotted a squad of NVA on the edge of the jungle and took them under fire. They fled up the hill towards where the 1/8th Recon patrol had been dropped. They had heard the contact and were ready for action. The enemy force entered the kill zone in their khaki-tan uniforms and the 1/8th opened fire, killing three NVA soldiers.

The others managed to escape and ran up the hill into the heavily forested hilltop. The 1/8th patrol advanced up the hill in search of them. This was standard operations for the enemy. Get us to chase them so they could lure us into a trap of machine-gun emplacements.

As the 1/8th Platoon slowly crept forward, they spotted enemy machine-gun positions up on a ridgeline under the trees. Unfortunately, the NVA also spotted them at that exact moment and opened fire. A deadly firefight ensued.

Down at the lower end of the hill, we heard the contact and rapidly moved up to join the 1/8th patrol. Together we launched an attack on the ridgeline positions, but we were driven back by heavy machine-gun fire. We called for fire support, giving the coordinates of the hilltop. After receiving this, we called for our gunships to roll in and work over the area.

Troop C gunships arrived on station and made a rocket and gun run on the enemy hilltop position, using the 1/8th patrol's smoke marker, strafing the ridgeline with rocket and machine-gun fire. Unfortunately, as happens in such close in fighting, a stray rocket hit the 1/8th position, wounding some of the men. So now we had wounded to care for.

The barrage was effective, however, and the NVA pulled back from the ridgeline further up the hill. Headquarters ordered us to collect our wounded and withdraw with the 1/8th to our LZs for extraction. Before we could reach the LZ darkness fell, and the enemy regrouped and mounted flanking attacks on us as we were carrying our wounded. A series of running firefights broke out along the trail all throughout the night. It was a run through hell. We took more wounded. For a while, it looked like we would be wiped out.

The aero lift platoon was sent in to rescue our embattled patrol. The lead helicopter, piloted by CWO Darwin Heffner and First Lieutenant Dan Honeywell, was badly damaged by enemy groundfire. Both pilots were severely wounded. Heffner passed out from loss of blood and Honeywell, bleeding heavily, managed to keep his bird airborne but could not land on the LZ. A gunship piloted by First Lieutenant Joe Waters and WO Gene Smith assisted Honeywell as he navigated his bird back to the Special Forces airstrip for a shaky landing. Lieutenant Waters had to use his landing light to illuminate the airstrip so the half-conscious Honeywell could complete the landing.

By dawn we had fought our way back to our LZ to find it had been secured by reinforcements. I think there was a unit from the 12th Cav at our LZ firing at the enemy to get them off our backs. Their big mortars were very effective in killing many of them and we were able to make it back; the enemy did not want to tangle with the 12th Cav as they knew they would get their asses kicked. Added to that, our Scouts and gunships were on station above us and were hunting down the enemy fleeing from the battlefield. It had been a long and deadly night on the move without any sleep or water. We were all exhausted from the ordeal, but we made it out alive, and we were very lucky to do so. Our wounded were evacuated by helicopters to a medical aid station set up along a coastal highway near Tuy Hoa. The operation's estimated final enemy body count was 134 after the 12th Cav had swept the area. A good day's work for the Air Cavalry. These were the kinds of patrols that would come back to haunt me years later. I would wake up from a nightmare, my heart pounding and my body covered in sweat, dreaming that I was still running through the jungle, firing my weapon in an effort to stop the enemy from overrunning our platoon. It was a damn miracle that I survived that patrol.

CHAPTER FOURTEEN

Hot Rod Pilot

Mike

Operation *Byrd*. In late August, Troop C was ordered to a coastal town called Phan Thiet to take part in an operation conducted by 2/7th Cavalry, with recon support by the 1/9th Air Cav, called *Task Force "Gary Owen."* We parked our helicopters in tactical formation near the airstrip and began to settle in to our new location. After digging foxholes and setting up our tents, my platoon set up the maintenance area for the upcoming missions. After Tuy Hoa, we knew all the sand meant extra work trying to keep the filters clean.

The next day, as we were having morning chow, a U.S. Army fixed-wing Beaver aircraft took off down the airstrip. As it got airborne, its engine began to sputter.

Everyone stopped to watch. We knew the pilot was in trouble. He was losing power. Instead of aborting take-off and trying to make a landing in the flat open land at the end of the airstrip, the plane, which was now about 100 feet up in the air, banked right in an effort to turn around. The engine stalled and the nose pointed straight down at the ground. The plane fell to the ground with a loud crash and a huge cloud of dust, but no fire or explosion.

"Holy shit!"

"Did you see that?"

"Somebody needs to get over there and help them!"

Everyone was shouting all at once. Some of the pilots ran to their helicopters and cranked up the engines so they could fly over to where the wreck was. Then a side door on the crashed plane opened, and a man jumped out. We all cheered. Then a second man jumped out. More cheers. Then the two men turned back to the aircraft and extracted a third man from the wreck. You would have thought we were watching a World Series baseball game as we were all cheering and yelling so wildly.

One of the Slicks took off and flew over to the three crewmen who had moved away from the wreckage. Nobody could believe they had all survived that crash. It was a testament to the sturdiness of the Canadian-built Beaver, for sure. The three men were picked up by the Slick and brought to a local field hospital for treatment. The Beaver was from a small Army aviation company under the command of MACV in Saigon.

There was always something happening out in the field. Not always good. We had our share of accidents that were sometimes fatal.

One afternoon, I accidentally shorted out a cable as I was replacing a battery on my bird when my wrench touched the metal framework of the tail boom. I burned my right hand and had to go to the squadron medical tent to get it treated by a doctor. I worried about getting an infection.

"That's a nasty burn you've got there, Kelley." The medic put some ointment on my hand and wrapped it up in a bandage. "Be careful with that. I've seen men put down with wounds like that if they aren't cared for properly." The medic gave me aspirin for the pain.

A few hours later, my hand started to throb. I took some aspirin, but it did not help the pain. I was removed from flight duty, but I still had to work on my aircraft, pulling inspections and making mechanical adjustments. I needed the relief from flying anyway.

One night, my buddy came back to our tent with a puppy. When we got into our sleeping bags and tucked our mosquito nets around us, the puppy came around to my side of the tent and laid against the mosquito net close to me. A few hours later I woke up feeling itchy, with a stinging sensation all over my face. I got out my flashlight and shined it on my arm. Bugs! Tiny bugs were crawling all over me. I shined my light onto the puppy and saw that it was covered with fleas.

"Wake up! This puppy is covered with fleas and they're eating me alive! You've got to move him!"

My tent mate sluggishly came to and moved the dog as I got out my insect repellent and washed my face, arms, and neck with the sticky lotion. It was not a comfortable night, and I tossed and turned until sunrise. The next day I aired out my sleeping bag and fumigated the tent with insect spray. The puppy got a bath with Army soap. It seemed to do the trick, as I didn't get bitten again.

The enemy occasionally lobbed mortars into our base and after the first few times, we began to improve our foxholes, making them deeper. The holes were expanded, and the men gathered empty, wooden ammo crates and used the lumber to build small roofs over them. A shelter half was secured on the top to seal out the rain. They were better than nothing.

One night at about 0200 hours the Viet Cong attacked our base, trying to penetrate the perimeter with sappers. They hit us with a heavy mortar attack. During the assault, I cut my hand open and it was bleeding pretty bad. I wrapped a towel around it and after the attack ended, I went to the medical tent to have them look at it. The medic put a compress on it, wrapped it up, and told me to come back the next day to see the doctor. By the time I had a doctor look at it, it was too late. It had gotten infected overnight and was now swelling and full of pus.

"You should have had this stitched up right away. That wound goes to the bone," the doctor told me as he patched me up. He gave me some antibiotics and more pain pills. I was in misery. Now I had a burned hand *and* a cut hand that would take much longer to heal in the humid, tropical air of Vietnam. Working on my helicopter became very painful. Turning wrenches and handling repair parts with two injured hands is not something I would wish on anyone. But this was war, and the maintenance of our aircraft was a number one priority. Painful hands or not, repairs went on.

The tempo of combat operations soon picked up as the 1/9th went out in support of the 2nd Battalion, 7th Cavalry's *Task Force Gary Owen*. "Gary Owen" was an old Irish drinking song that the horse cavalry troops sung back in the late 1800s. Many of the cavalrymen in those Indian War days were freed Black slaves or veterans of the Civil War. Some were Irish immigrants. Now their descendants were fighting in the same Army, but in a new war.

The 2/7th was tasked with clearing and securing an area of about 5,000 miles in the province. The local Viet Cong units were the 482nd and 840th Battalions and they had been operating in the area without any interference from the South Vietnamese government. The 2/7th Task Force was about to spoil their party.

In cooperation with the Luong Son Special Forces Detachment of the 5th Special Forces Group, a series of air assaults were initiated in and around the Le Fong Forest to flush out the enemy from their fortified base camps. As the 2/7th Cavalry made combat sweeps in different locations to box the enemy in, the Scouts and gunships of the 1st of the 9th flew reconnaissance missions to locate, find, and fix Viet Cong positions. The Blues were inserted to carry out ground searches to follow up on contacts made by the Scouts. As the 2/7th put pressure on the enemy, the Scouts flew low-level screening missions to track the enemy down and cut them off as they tried to escape.

In one battle, the Scouts spotted a number of Viet Cong soldiers northwest of Phan Thiet and engaged them in a running firefight. The VC retreated to a bunker complex and the Blues went in to determine the strength of the enemy force. A sharp, fierce battle ensued, and a high volume of fire was exchanged. The gunships went in to provide rocket and machine-gun suppressive fire. Then, having fixed the enemy position, the 1/9th called in the 2/7th for backup and two platoons of infantry were air assaulted in by the 227th Assault Helicopter Battalion to join the battle. The 2/20th Aerial Rocket Artillery was called in to work over the VC bunker complex. This fight ended with 52 Viet Cong dead, and one American KIA.

By the time Operation *Byrd* ended, the Viet Cong were neutralized in the province. National Highway Route 1 was reopened to Saigon for commerce. The 2/7th reported 481 enemy dead and 70 captured. They also captured 151 weapons and 291 tons of rice. 600 enemy fortifications and bunkers were destroyed, with a loss of 11 Americans KIA. On January 17, 1973, President Richard Nixon awarded the 2/7th Task Force the Presidential Unit Citation, including all attached units, for conspicuous gallantry and heroism.

Before Operation *Byrd* ended, I was called to the command post tent to see our new first sergeant. I think his last name was Sumari. He was from American Samoa. A big, good-natured guy who looked like a native warrior. I entered his tent and reported as ordered.

"Sit down, Kelley."

I did as he said. For a few seconds he just sat there, looking at me with a smile on his face. *What is he smiling about?*

"Kelley, you have been out in the field longer than any of the other men in the platoon. I've decided to send you back to An Khe. They need a crew chief for a helicopter that is being used to train new pilots."

His news was completely unexpected. I couldn't believe my ears. "Get your gear and catch the next plane out of here!" He waved me off. I stood up and walked out of the tent.

I was being sent back to the rear area! No more field operations. I quickly went back to my tent and gave away all the extra field gear I had accumulated to my buddies. Then I packed up what was left and walked over to the airstrip. An Army aviation company was operating some Army CV-2 Caribou cargo planes there. I got my name on the flight manifest and climbed onto the aircraft for the flight back to An Khe Base Camp. It felt great leaving the field for the rear.

The crew aboard the CV-2 was a mixed bag. There was an Army chief warrant officer pilot and an Army crew chief. The other pilot was an Air Force captain, and with him was an Air Force cargo master. The Army crew chief told us that the Air Force was taking over operations of all CV-2 aircraft and they were learning how to fly and operate the aircraft from the Army crewmen.

Upon landing at An Khe, the front tire blew out and the plane veered to the right of the runway, almost going into a ditch. *That was close.* We got off the plane shortly after, walking down the rear ramp.

"That Air Force pilot sure made a hard landing," the Army crew chief joked as he exited the plane.

The rear area for Troop C was like a ghost town. Most of the troop was out at Phan Thiet and there was only a small detachment of soldiers assigned to the rear. A few worked in the orderly room, others were in unit supply, and a few were pulling odd details, like cutting grass in front of squadron headquarters or painting rocks along the walkway. I would come to find out that most of these men were on light duty as a result of wounds or injuries.

The first thing I had to do upon arriving was report to the new executive officer, a major.

"Specialist Kelley reporting for duty, sir!"

"You're out of uniform, soldier!"

Damn, I've only been back for a half hour and already the Army chickenshit is at work.

"What do you mean, sir?"

The major opened a drawer and pulled out a pair of SP5 stripes and pushed them across his desk towards me.

"That's what I mean, soldier. You're an E-5 now."

I picked up the stripes, dumbfounded.

"I don't understand why I am getting these stripes, sir."

"Your first sergeant put you in for promotion. He said you deserve these stripes. So next time I see you, I want these on you. Understand?"

"Yes sir!" I gave him a smart hand salute and left his office walking on a cloud. I couldn't believe my luck. First, my new top sergeant relieves me from field duty and gives me a cushy job in the rear, and then he adds the icing on the cake by making me an E-5. My bad luck was starting to change, and I was now, as the veterans would say, "In the rear, with the beer!"

That night, I went up the hill to drink at the NCO Club for the first time. You had to be an E-5 to get in. I sat down to drink my beer, and it didn't take me long to realize that I was in there with the "Lifers," the career men. All of the soldiers in there were older than me. I was only 20 and they were all in their late 20s to mid-30s. We used to call them old men back then.

I went back to my hootch and changed into my jacket with the E-4 rank. Then I headed over to the Enlisted Men's (EM) Club, where all the action was. It was loud and smoky, with rock and roll playing from a speaker on the wall. You could always count on meeting someone you knew, and a few fights to liven things up. It was a lot more fun than the NCO Club.

That night, I slept on my metal Army cot in my hootch. A big improvement over sleeping in a pup tent or a fortified foxhole out in the field with the snakes and creepy crawlies.

The only problem we really had to deal with at the rear were the rats that were almost as big as cats. They invaded the hootches and the supply tent at night, getting into the 50-pound burlap bags of rice, flour, and other foodstuffs. All good pickings for vermin.

I got a few rat traps from unit supply and set them out at night with some cheese spread from my C-ration box. During the night, the rats ran across the rafters of the hootch, scurried up and down the beams along the walls and across the cement floor. One night, a rat crashed into my tin wash pan on the floor, knocking it clear across the room. In the mornings, I always found a few victims in my traps. They had eaten their last free meal. The guys who walked by my hootch and saw me carrying the traps outside to bury the dead rats called me the "Pied Piper of An Khe."

I wasn't about to mess around, though. The four-legged creatures were a major health threat. If they bit you, the doctor had to give you a series of special shots to curtail the infection. That was not for me. At night, in addition to the traps, I hung my mosquito net over my bunk and tucked the ends under my sleeping bag. Then I sprayed around my sleeping bag with insect repellent for an extra line of defense. Those rats weren't going to get me!

In the field, we had to contend with snakes and spiders. At base camp, it was rats and Viet Cong mortars. There was always something extra to make our lives miserable.

I reported to the headquarters troop maintenance tent down at the Golf Course for duty. The maintenance NCO assigned me to a worn-out OH-13S Scout helicopter and gave me the list of repairs it needed to become flightworthy. As I ran my inspection, my new pilot showed up to find out the status of the bird. First Lieutenant Robert Franklin was about 25 years old, with a stocky build and a great smile.

He was a Scout pilot with extensive low-level recon experience. I liked him right away.

Because we were both combat veterans, we knew the drill. The bird had to be flight ready every day. Lieutenant Franklin had the responsibility of taking new pilots up and training them in the art of 1st Cavalry style combat flying, using NOE techniques, also known as contour flying. He showed them how to keep the bird in flight while using the trees and terrain to hide the aircraft from sight to avoid groundfire. My new old bird had dual flight controls, perfect for the mission. The combat Scout birds only had single flight controls, so the observer-gunner had clearance to fire his weapons easier.

Within a few days, I had the old bird in flying status. I had to replace the hydraulic servos, all the flight control cables from front to rear, a bell crank, pitch links, a fuel tank, and the tail rotor hub. All that was left for it was a flight test from a pilot.

That afternoon, Lieutenant Franklin showed up for the test flight.

"Grab a flight helmet, Kelley, you're coming with me."

I had been on many test flights before, so I grabbed my helmet unconcerned.

After Franklin performed his pre-flight inspection, we climbed in and fired up the engine. The rotors slowly came to life and within a few minutes we were off the ground and gaining altitude over base camp, heading north over the expanse of the jungle. We were on a single ship mission, so if anything went wrong and we went down, we were in big trouble. I felt a little uncomfortable to be flying without a backup bird and I looked over the instruments to ensure everything was working okay.

"How is she handling, lieutenant?" Once I confirmed the instruments indicated all was well, I wanted to see how Franklin felt.

"So far it's running smooth. No vibrations. Let's take it down for some low-level flight."

He immediately dropped us into a steep, left-bank turn and headed down towards the trees. We dropped down to tree-top level and he put on some power in forward flight. We zoomed along just inches above the treetops at 60 knots. When we came to a tall tree, he flipped us sideways and kept on rolling. Then we came to an open field where he set the bird down. *I sure hope there aren't any VC snipers in the area, we're sitting ducks in this field. What is he doing?*

Lieutenant Franklin pushed the cyclic forward and added some power. The bird stood up on its front skids and bumped along the ground like a bunny rabbit hopping. Finally, it lifted off the ground and we gained air speed, climbing back to about 50 feet. Franklin looked at me and smiled. *Good, he seems pleased. Maybe now we can head back to base camp.*

Then Franklin took us back down on the treetops and opened up the collective throttle. It wasn't long before we were flying along at 75 knots! Our skids hit the trees below us, tearing off branches and leaves. *This test flight is turning into one wild ride!* In all of my combat recon missions, I never had a Scout pilot fly through the trees like Lieutenant Franklin. He seemed intent on showing off his skills with low-level flying.

We came to an open field full of tall elephant grass and he began to drag our skids through its green vastness. *If there are any hidden anthills in this grass and we hit one, we're dead.* I was really starting to get uncomfortable. As we approached the tree line, he kept us at ground level while maintaining plenty of airspeed. I looked at the trees coming towards us. *What is he doing?* I was just about to yell at him when he rolled the bird sideways and we slipped through an opening between two large trees. Our main rotor blades chopped off branches like a big lawnmower. *That's it! I've had enough!*

"Lieutenant! What the hell are you doing?"

He looked over at me with a huge grin. "What's wrong?"

"I've been through too much combat to get killed flying like this!"

"Okay, Kelley. We can call it a day."

"You fly like a hot rod pilot. I've never seen any other commissioned officer fly like that. It's usually the younger WO pilots who do that. I'm not trying to die now at the end of my tour of duty."

"Sorry, I didn't mean to scare you. I just like flying like that. I used to drive a 64 GTO when I was in college before I joined the Army and I always liked driving it fast. It's fun for me."

"Well, it's not fun for me!"

When we got back to the flight line, I was very happy to have my feet on the ground. I thought of all the new pilots that would be training with Lieutenant Franklin and I was glad that I was not one of them.

After I got my aircraft mechanically sound, I began to work on the paint. It was worn out; faded, chipped, and scratched all over. I tried to obtain a can of regulation olive drab green paint, but no one had any to spare. I knew that somewhere in Vietnam there was a whole warehouse full of that olive drab paint, but we had none. So, I did what any enterprising young man would do. I made my own.

I went down to the village of An Khe and found a little paint shop where I bought a can of dark green and a can of yellow paint. I mixed the paint until the color was close to the olive drab green of the Army issue paint. But I didn't think about the fact that the paint I had just purchased had a gloss finish. When I finished painting the bird it looked much different than a regulation 1st Cav OH-13.

It wasn't long before the mechanics at headquarters troop nicknamed that bird the "Green Hornet." The clearly non-regulation color caused my pilot to get a lot of comments from other pilots and officers about his bird.

Soon, I was called into the headquarters maintenance tent.

"Kelley, a high-ranking officer from division headquarters wants to know why your bird is painted that color."

"It needed paint, sir, and I was told there wasn't any available, so I tried to make my own."

"Well, a gallon of paint has now been located. Go pick it up and paint your aircraft the proper color."

I went over to the 15th Maintenance Battalion and was issued a gallon of the Army olive drab green paint. It took a few days, but I finally had my bird painted like a 1st Cav helicopter.

Lieutenant Franklin found a spot to land and park my bird that was up on the hill near the officers' hootches. I did not like this. The spot was on the rear slope of the hill, which was an isolated area that looked down over the perimeter at the back of base camp. When I went up there early in the morning to perform pre-flight inspections, I was alone and a perfect target for a VC sniper who could fire from the tree line about 1,000 meters away. As a "short-timer" with less than 90 days left in Vietnam, I was nervous. I let my pilot know how I felt, but he assured me that the area was safe. I still did not like it.

One day I was called to the Troop C orderly room. My old request for a three-day leave to visit my sister down at Nha Trang had been approved. I checked with headquarters troop and the maintenance NCO said one of his mechanics would take care of my bird while I was gone. Once I got permission from Lieutenant Franklin, I packed my bag and headed to the airfield where I caught an Air Force C-130 cargo plane headed to Nha Trang.

When I arrived, I spotted a snack bar and went inside to get something to eat. I was flabbergasted by what I saw. They had a stateside-type grill and counter setup where you could order hamburgers and beer. I quickly ordered both. As I was eating, a couple of Air Force guys entered the snack bar and sat next to me. After ordering a cold drink, they turned to me.

"Where are you coming from, soldier?"

"I'm with the 1st Cavalry, just in on a short leave for a visit with my sister."

"1st Cavalry, huh? You guys get quite a bit of action out there." He turned to the guy behind the counter. "This guy's 1st Cav. We'll pick up his tab, okay?"

"Thanks. You don't have to do that."

"Don't think about it. You guys deserve it."

We sat and chatted for a bit while I ate. As I finished up, the second guy turned to me. "We can give you a ride into Nha Trang if you'd like."

"Sure, it makes it easier on me that way. Thanks again."

"No problem."

As we drove along by the airfield, I spotted a line of AC-47 Douglas gunships.

"Is that a Spooky?"

"Yeah, a whole line of them right there."

"Wow. It sure would be great to get a closer look at one of those."

"No problem. We can make that happen."

They turned their Air Force pickup truck onto the runway and drove up to the aircraft. One of them walked up to the maintenance crew.

"Hey, he's here visiting us from the 1st Cav. He wants to have a closer look at this aircraft here. Is that good?"

"Okay, sure. That's fine."

I walked around and took a couple of color pictures of the famous aircraft that I had seen in action up in Bong Son. These planes were from the 4th Air Commando Squadron, which consisted of 20 AC-47D gunships. These aircraft were equipped with three 7.62mm SUU-11A Gatling mini-guns with 16,500 rounds of ammo. They were an awesome sight during a nighttime attack on enemy targets with their high rate of fire and long bursts of red tracer fire. I remembered one support mission in particular at Bong Son where a Spooky gunship provided suppressive fires and illumination firing at a hilltop Viet Cong bunker position where they killed an estimated 300 Viet Cong.

The Air Force guys drove me to the edge of town and from there I hitched a ride in an Army Jeep with a full bird colonel driving it.

"What unit are you with, son?" he asked me as I climbed in and got settled.

"The 1st of the 9th, sir."

"Oh, you're one of Jim Smith's boys!" LTC James Smith was the commander of the 1/9th. It seemed as though my unit got me an in with everyone I met in Nha Trang.

The colonel drove me into town where I checked into a hotel for my three-day visit. I called my sister at the 8th Field Hospital and she arrived within the hour in a civilian CJ Jeep painted baby blue. She had a couple of her nurse friends with her.

"Hey Michael, good to see you!" She gave me a big hug. "Get your bag, check out of the hotel. You don't need to stay here. I'm going to set you up with living quarters on my base."

"You don't need to do that, I'm fine here, rea…"

"No, come on. You're coming with me."

"But I wanted to live in town and…"

"Michael. Don't argue. You're coming with me."

That was that. I really had wanted to live in town and explore the area on my own, but she had already made up her mind. I checked out and climbed into the baby blue Jeep and we went to the 8th Field Hospital compound across town. When we got to the compound, my big sister took me to her first sergeant.

"Good afternoon, Sergeant. This is my brother, Michael. He's visiting for a few days from the 1st Cavalry. You think you could put him up until he goes back?"

"Yeah, sure. I have some medics on TDY, so I've got a few empty bunks that he can use."

I ended up sleeping in a big Quonset hut barracks with a Vietnamese housemaid who shined my boots and made my bed. This was something we never saw with the 1st Cavalry as no Vietnamese were even allowed on our base camp. I thought I wouldn't see any fun while I was at Nha Trang, but I was wrong. The medics took me downtown that night and we had a great time drinking and raising hell.

My sister was off duty one of the afternoons I was there, and she took me to a fine seaside French restaurant. We dined on all sorts of food, but I had no idea what I was eating. On the way back, we were walking along the seaside roadway. She was wearing civilian clothes and I was wearing my fatigues with my sleeves rolled up over my E-5 stripes. My cap had a pair of silver aircrewman wings and the shiny gold unit emblem of the 1/9th Cavalry. All the Army Jeeps and trucks that drove by saluted us. I realized that I must have looked like an officer pilot with the rank of a major.

"Michael, you have to stop saluting at these guys. They all think you're an officer. Enlisted men do not walk with nurse officers."

My sister seemed to be embarrassed, but I was having a ball impersonating an officer. None of the soldiers in the Jeeps knew that they were really just saluting a lowly SP5.

My sister and her nurse friends lived in a nice civilian-style villa on the compound. They had a living room and private bedrooms. It was a far cry from the dirty conditions of field duty. This was officers' country.

That night they had a party and I met many of her fellow officers, doctors, nurses, and support staff. They all thought it was unusual that she had a younger brother who was an enlisted man. They brought food and drinks and we all had a good time. Because I stayed late, my sister had me sleep in a bunk bed that belonged to one of the nurses who was on duty that night. The experience of waking up in a bed of clean, white sheets that smelled faintly of perfume was quite strange after all my time spent in the field.

It was a sad day when I had to say goodbye to my sister. My parents worried greatly with both of us in the war zone, and I would be going home in a few months and leaving her in Vietnam. I caught another Air Force flight back to my base at An Khe in the Central Highlands and went back to my duties as crew chief on the Green Hornet.

During the month of October, the 9th Cavalry was engaged in combat operations when Alpha and Charlie Troops were deployed to Bong Son. Alpha Troops Scouts spotted seven Viet Cong in the seacoast village of Hoa Hoi and their troop commander's Huey gunship went in and shot all seven of them before they could escape. The Blues were inserted, and they quickly came under heavy fire from enemy fortified positions. PFC John Weigart attacked a hidden .51mm cal heavy machine gun that was firing at the Blues. He killed the two gunners using hand grenades and his .45mm cal pistol.

The commander's gunship attacked another .51mm cal machine gun, knocking it out with cross machine-gun fire. SP5 Larry Wright and PFC Robert Andrews got out on the skids and fired their M-60 door guns at the Viet Cong, killing 30 of the enemy. The village was laced with fortified bunkers and trenches, and fire came from every direction.

PFC Lynn Gaylord saw a machine-gun position that no one else had spotted yet. He stood up to draw its fire, so the rest of the squad could see it in action. He was shot in the shoulder, but it enabled his squad to destroy the machine gun with 18 hand grenades.

As the 4th Squad advanced across the village, heavy machine-gun fire pinned them down. Gunships came in and raked the VC with rocket and machine-gun fire. The commander's gunship positioned his aircraft between the squad and the machine gun, allowing the pinned down squad to move to a better position with their wounded.

The gunship then moved to pick up a seriously wounded medic. As they loaded the medic on the helicopter, the co-pilot, Lieutenant Pat Haley, spotted a lone enemy soldier coming up behind the aircraft. He swung the aircraft to the side and the tail boom hit the enemy, killing him. Under heavy fire, the gunship lifted off, only to come under more withering ground fire. The badly damaged ship barely managed to fly back to the LZ.

A Scout team located twin enemy machine-gun positions, and despite heavy damage to their aircraft, they managed to drop hand grenades on one gun and marked the other with smoke for the gunships to locate and attack it with rockets. The gunships knocked out both machine-gun positions. The wounded Scout aircraft made it back to the LZ, setting down next to the commander's damaged gunship.

By 1100 hours, the 1st Battalion, 12th Cavalry arrived to take over the battle. More than 200 of the enemy were killed in Operation *Irving*, and the 1/9th received the Presidential Unit Citation for this action. Once again, the 1st of the 9th had found and fixed the enemy for the division.

CHAPTER FIFTEEN

In Memory of Our Commander

Anyone who has ever played football will tell you that the team's success on the field hinges on the capabilities of its quarterback. The quarterback is the commanding officer of his team, and if he is skillful and good under pressure, his team will be victorious.

That analogy is the best I can think of to describe my commanding officer, Major Billy Joe Nave. He wasn't just someone who was skillful and good under pressure. He also led by example, and he expected his officers and non-commissioned officers to do the same. He was a fair but firm leader, and most importantly, he was a soldier's soldier. He had a special affection for his enlisted men. Even though he called us all by our last names when addressing us, he knew every single one of us by our first name.

One day, Major Nave received a new UH-1C Huey gunship to replace his old B model that had been shot down at Bong Son. I was working on my helicopter when he came up to me.

"Kelley, how would you like to be a PFC again?"

I stopped what I was doing to look at him. He had a big grin on his face. At the time I was a SP4, one pay grade above PFC, so I didn't understand what he meant.

"What do you mean, sir?"

He pointed to his new Huey. "If you don't paint that design on the nose of my bird, you will be a PFC again."

A week earlier he had given me a sketch on a piece of paper to paint on his gunship, since he knew it was something I was good at. It was a huge horseshoe magnet with electronic rays drawing up groundfire (bullets) towards the magnet. I had been so busy keeping my helicopter flight ready that I had forgotten. I realized he was joking.

"I will get on that right away, sir!"

He patted me on the shoulder. "Good man!" Then he walked away to take care of more important business.

I collected my homemade painting kit that I had stored in an old M-16 ammo can. Then I went over to his new Huey and began to draw a rough outline with a number two pencil. The design would stand out on the flat black paint of the Huey's nose.

I painted a large oval with light mint-green enamel as the background. When that dried, I began painting out the details of the sketch. A large horseshoe magnet, facing down, with electronic rays drawing bullets up towards it. Just the way he wanted it.

A few hours later, Major Nave came by to check on my progress. Thankfully he was pleased with the results. I didn't have to worry about becoming a PFC again. The major soon garnered the nickname "Old Magnet Ass" by the troops.

One of the things I liked about Major Nave was that he had a good sense of humor and was easy to talk to. Back in that era, there was an unofficial Army rule that you were not to speak to officers and senior NCOs unless they initiated the conversation, a sort of caste system. Lowly enlisted men who were under the pay grade level of E-5 were considered peons who needed to just keep their mouths shut and do their jobs.

Most of the time we would go out on missions and have no idea where we were going or why we were going there. We did not have the need to know. Our pilot officers, for the most part, did not tell us what was going on, although there were some exceptions. Some officers were very friendly and engaged us in conversations, some even asked us for our opinions. Major Nave was like that.

He was well liked by everyone in the troop, from the highest-ranking officers to the lowest PFC. We would do anything for him, would follow him to hell and back if asked.

When we were working out of the Dak To–Kontum area near the Cambodian border, we were in pretty desperate in need of clothing supplies. A lot of supplies were being stolen from supply ships and being sold on the black market. Many of us field troopers were dealing with worn-out green fatigues, disintegrated underwear, and boots that were falling apart, with missing heels that had peeled off from the moisture and jungle rot. The 1st Cav's supply system was lacking everything from aircraft hydraulic servos to underwear at the time. We were pretty disheartened by the situation. Keep in mind, logistics was in its infancy for the cav in 1966.

One day, the supply sergeant arrived on the daily resupply helicopter from An Khe loaded with cardboard boxes full of clothing supplies. When he told everyone he had a free issue of jungle boots and fatigues and began to give them out, we all lined up quickly. Before long, a bunch of officers had moved to the front of the line to ensure they got their free issue.

When Major Nave showed up and saw what was going on, he went to the front of the line and ordered everyone to return their free issue to the supply sergeant.

"No one is to get anything until all the Blues get their fatigues and boots. Then the enlisted men go next, then the sergeants. Officers get their free issue last."

The men who had already received their free issue immediately returned the items to the supply sergeant and went to the back of the line as ordered.

Major Nave was keenly aware of the morale and welfare of his enlisted men, especially his elite infantrymen, and he was determined to maintain good morale within his troops. That day, he displayed the command style that we all admired and respected him for. He was a good and fair commander, but more than that, he was a good man.

Major Billy Joe Nave was born on November 29, 1933. He grew up in Johnson City, Tennessee, in the northeast part of the state, not far from the beautiful Blue Ridge Mountains. There a boy could hunt in the valleys and fish in the rivers, and the rapid white waters were perfect for rafting and kayaking in the summer.

As a teenager, Billy Joe had attended Science Hill High School, where he was a member of the Hill Topper Cadet Program of the Junior

R.O.T.C. program. In the early 1950s, he attended East Tennessee State University, where he was a popular student. He was active with the Mu Epsilon Nu fraternity and held the rank of cadet major in the Pershing Rifles R.O.T.C. program. Billy Joe graduated in June 1955 and was commissioned as a 2nd Lieutenant in the Army Reserve. He chose to pursue a military career after college and was sent to Fort Benning, Georgia to attend infantry officer school. He completed his training there in December 1955. He then went on to ranger school, which he graduated from in February 1956.

That same year he met and married his wife Nan in Chattanooga, Tennessee. In 1957, he attended Army pilot training school at Fort Rucker, where he learned how to fly both fixed wing and rotary wing aircraft. While there, his first child, Terri, was born.

From then on, Billy Joe was sent on an assortment of assignments as an Army aviator. He went to Germany, Korea, and a number of stateside duty stations. In 1960, his second child, William Joe, was born. The little family traveled the world in support of their father's career.

In 1964, Captain Nave arrived at the new experimental Air Cavalry unit at Fort Benning, known as the 11th Air Assault Division (TEST). There he met and trained with the future leaders of the famous 1st Cavalry Division (AIRMOBILE), men such as John B. Stockton, Robert M. Shoemaker, and James C. Smith. His new unit, the 3rd Squadron, 17th Cavalry (that would later become known as the 1st Squadron, 9th Cavalry), was tasked with the mission of aerial reconnaissance for the division. They became known as "the Eyes and Ears of the Cav."

Due to the long periods of time spent in the field on Airmobile operations, Billy Joe did not have much quality time with his family. Like many military families, they sacrificed their quality time for the good of their country's national defense.

Terri remembers one time when her father managed to break away from his demanding training schedule to come home during the afternoon and sit by her bed, feeding her a bowl of chicken soup. She was sick with the mumps. She still has the image of him sitting there in his green Army fatigues with his white aviator wings.

On June 27, 1966, Army officers knocked on the door of the Naves' Fort Benning apartment to inform the family that Billy Joe had been killed in a helicopter crash in Vietnam. Terri remembers the shock as they were overwhelmed by a sea of grief. Her mother was devastated that day; Nan never got over the terrible loss of her husband. She carried the love she had for him in her heart for the rest of her life. The tragic loss of a young husband and father resulted in a life-long sorrow that the family had to endure.

The loss of Billy Joe Nave was also felt by his beloved soldiers of Charlie Troop who survived the war. The major was gone, but he would never be forgotten by those who loved him. His memory will live on in these pages for future generations to know who this wonderful man was, and how he touched so many lives in his short time on this earth.

The story of Charlie Troop 65–66 is the story of a star quarterback who led his team to many victories on the field of battle in Vietnam. Major Billy Joe Nave was Charlie Troop's quarterback, and he lived and fought for his men. We, his troopers, lived and fought for him. We were an elite team, and we followed our squadron's motto:

"We Can, We Will."

For we were the Air Cavalry Recon. The eyes and the ears of the 1st Cavalry Division.

Epilogue

Mike

By November 1, I was down to almost 30 days left on my tour of duty. My buddy, PFC Peter Burbank, had less than that.

Back at base camp, we received our orders to return home. Those orders were known as DEROS, short for Date Return from Overseas. Within a few days we began the paper process called clearing post, where you had a checklist that had to be signed by every section in the troop to make sure you returned equipment and received medical and administrative clearance to go home.

Back then, we had a saying for short timers. "I'm so short, I can jump off a dime!" We were in the mood to celebrate. At the time, there were about a half a dozen guys who were getting ready to go home. In the evenings we would all meet up by my hootch to hang out and talk about what we were going to do when we got stateside.

For the last few weeks in Vietnam we partied almost every night. We were a happy crew, knowing that we had less than 30 days left in country. The best day was when I turned in my aircraft toolbox to the supply shop and was officially relieved from duty as a crew chief. I had survived my long combat tour and test flight with Lieutenant Franklin.

It was hard to believe I was going home.

On December 1, the day George was killed out at Bong Son, First Sergeant Sumari returned to the rear base camp at An Khe and came into my hootch. All of us short-timers were there, hanging out and drinking beer. He sat down, and we offered him one. As he sipped his brew, he told us about the day's events. Then came the big question.

"The troop commander sent me here to ask you boys if any of you would consider extending your departure for a week. The troop has been hit hard; we lost some men, including George Gavaria. And there were a lot of wounded, so we are shorthanded."

We all looked at each other warily as he finished his beer and stood up to leave.

"You don't have to decide now. Think it over and let me know tomorrow." Then he left us to ponder the thought of returning to the war. It was a difficult night for all of us, knowing that our buddies were out there under fire and we were going home. Part of us wanted to return with the 1st sergeant, but deep down inside, we all just really wanted to go home. We had survived, and it was time for us to go.

In the morning, the first sergeant returned to find out what we had decided. To a man, we told him we wanted to go home.

"I understand your feelings, boys. I had to ask, but I understand." He then gave us a case of beer. "Thank you for your year of service, men. Have a safe trip home."

Then he left and headed back to Bong Son on the re-supply bird. It was all over. That night we drank the beer from the first sergeant with great sadness, filled with survivor's guilt, but knowing we were free to leave the war zone.

On December 2, we packed our stuff and caught the flight from the An Khe Air strip out to Pleiku Air Base where we were processed and placed on a flight roster to go stateside. That night we slept in a large GP tent on cots and ate our last meal in Vietnam. The next morning, on December 3, 1966, we watched the huge Air Force C-141 Starlifter roll up to the ramp. As about 100 veteran soldiers lined up to load onboard the huge transport, another 100 men came out of the back of the plane and passed by us. *New meat for the war.* I was glad to be on the other side.

We climbed aboard the C-141 and took our seats in the cargo bay. The ramp came up and closed, and the bird powered up and rolled out to the runway for take-off. As it rumbled down the long, paved runway, everyone held their breath waiting for the plane to get off the ground and climb into the sky, away from the nightmare of Vietnam. After a few minutes, the pilot came on the intercom.

"Gentlemen, we have now left Vietnam airspace."

A great cheer erupted as we were all relieved to be out of the war zone for good.

As the jet streaked across the ocean, we settled in for our 18-hour flight home. We were given a small cardboard box containing a sandwich, milk, an apple, and a cookie. At about 0300 hours, we landed at Tachikowa Air Force Base in Japan to refuel and change crews. They put us in a big aircraft hangar and served us hot coffee. The airmen were wearing heavy parkas with fur hoods, as it was very cold there. We were all shivering in our short-sleeve, khaki, summer uniforms.

The next day we arrived at Travis Air Force Base in California and were taken by bus to the Oakland Army Base to be processed home on leave. At Oakland, we got a hot shower, a hot steak meal, a haircut, and a new Class A dress uniform. We also received a debriefing by a major. We were told not to talk to any media about our tour in Vietnam.

Around midnight, I was given an airline ticket and released. I caught a cab to the San Francisco Airport with some other guys and boarded a red-eye flight to Boston, via Dallas and Chicago. I was going home!

Within 24 hours, I was at Boston's Logan Airport where my brother picked me up and took me home to my old neighborhood, where the street was covered with snow. Just hours before, I had been in tropical Vietnam. Now, I was on my street, the street I had left on August 17, 1964, a little over two years prior. It was surreal and I found it hard to believe that I was really home.

What I did not know was that a new war was about to begin. This would be an internal war, the war of survivor's guilt and post-traumatic stress disorder.

My parents, my family, and my friends were happy to see me. I was home in time for Christmas. I took my backpay and drafted my brother George into helping me find a new car. We found a 1965 Chevy Super Sport 327 four speed at a car dealer in Boston and drove it home. It was the first real late-model car I ever owned. A far cry from my old 1951 Mercury from high school and Fort Belvoir.

After a 30-day leave filled with parties and old friends, I left East Cambridge once more for the long drive down to Fort Hood, Texas, where I had been reassigned. My cousin, Douglas D.P. Ryan, volunteered to help me drive my new Chevy to Texas. We took a side trip to visit his father in Detroit and his brother Robert, who had just completed training in the Air Force. From Detroit, we traveled through a heavy blizzard to sunny Fort Hood, Texas.

At Fort Hood, I reported in to my new unit, the 502nd Aviation Battalion, 2nd Armored Division. I was given a position as a UH-1H Huey crew chief on a brand-new helicopter. While I was there, I met many Vietnam veterans who had returned stateside like me to finish off their enlistments. Half of the men in our unit were veterans and the other half were new guys just out of aviation training school, waiting to ship overseas.

While at Fort Hood, I got to witness the Army testing out a new helicopter, the AH-1 Huey Cobra Gunship. By the end of 1967, that helicopter would start shipping to Vietnam to replace the older UH-1B gunships. My prior unit, the 9th Air Cavalry, would make the Cobra famous in Vietnam.

On August 16, 1967, I was discharged from the U.S. Army. It took me three days to drive back home to East Cambridge. Upon my arrival, I placed my uniform in the closet with plans to put the war behind me. I didn't realize that I would be back in uniform in a few years, dealing with the effects of the early stages of PTSD. The war never ended for me.

The summer of 1967 is well known as the Summer of Love. My hometown of Cambridge became the center of the anti-war movement on the East Coast. Harvard Square, at the center of the vast Harvard University campus, was a magnet for war protesters, hippies, and others drawn to the counterculture movement.

My home was only a few miles from the hotbed of protests and sit-ins that were occurring every week. Thousands of people marched through the square with signs saying, "Stop the War!" They shouted constant anti-government slogans.

This was a very difficult time for me. I found myself surrounded by people who did not support my service in Vietnam. It even affected my social life. Some of the girls I dated were supportive of the hippie agenda and I soon found myself alone, as I didn't want to deal with the anti-war atmosphere.

I drifted from one low-paying job to another, wondering how it was that I had once been a highly skilled aircraft technician in the Army and now I was working for only $2.50 an hour. I had been responsible for a million-dollar aircraft and now I was a nobody. I tried applying for better jobs with no luck. I applied to be a technician at the Boston Navy Yard. Rejected. I applied to be a mechanic at Logan International Airport but was told I needed an Aircraft and Powerplant certification.

By 1969, I managed to get a job as a ground equipment servicer at Logan airport. On my lunch hours, I went down to the lobby to greet returning servicemen as they got off the jet planes. This was my first contact with other Vietnam veterans. I felt a strong bond with them and wanted to let them know that someone cared about their service. Back then, it was as though we were all isolated from each other and surrounded by countrymen who didn't care about the sacrifices we had made. Even the Veterans Administration didn't understand the effects of the war on us yet. There was no PTSD outreach back then to help the war veterans.

After two and a half years of working in low paying jobs or living off unemployment checks, my brother George got me to take the examination for the U.S. Post Office. He was concerned about my future and felt an obligation to help me. After all, it was his advice that had prompted me to enlist in the U.S. Army and subsequently I got sent to Vietnam. If he had known, he might not have encouraged me to enlist. But how was he supposed to know that President Johnson would escalate the war in June 1965?

Things began to look up for me. On November 1, 1969, I was hired by the Post Office and began my government career. I met a local girl named Ruth, who was not involved in the anti-war movement. We enjoyed a good relationship and were soon engaged to be married. By late 1970, I was a married man with a decent job. But the war still haunted me. I felt a strong urge to rejoin my comrades in arms in Vietnam.

In December 1970, I took the Army induction physical exam at the Boston Army Base. I was told by my Army recruiter that I would be sent to Fort Rucker to be a technical instructor if I enlisted for three years. But my new wife and her family were concerned that I would be deployed back to Vietnam and objected to my desire to reenlist. But I didn't want to lose my opportunity to rejoin the military, so I took the next best option and enlisted into the U.S. Army Reserve for six years. This allowed me to keep my government job and serve with part-time soldiers on the weekend. In July 1971, our first child Michael Jr. was born, and we began to raise a family of two boys, Michael Jr. and Richard, who was born on April 23, 1975, just as the Vietnam War was ending with the communists' defeat of South Vietnam. It was an agonizing experience for me, but the joy of our baby boy helped me deal with the shock of the war's outcome, especially after all of our sacrifices to defend South Vietnam. Our daughter Jennifer (Genifa) completed our little family in July 1977. She was my princess.

Because of my prior service experience, the Army Reserve rapidly advanced me to staff sergeant (platoon sergeant). Then my life took a strange twist. In 1972, as the Army began to reorganize and become the new All Volunteer Army, they developed a recruiting program that was intended to locate prior service personnel and enlist them into the Army Reserve. The draft had been a big recruiting tool for the Army Reserve, and now that the draft was ending, they would need to compete for enlistees. This new program was called Project Search. The plan was to hire 10 Vietnam veterans and place them in major cities where they would work out of the Veterans Administration Center to interview and enlist interested veterans.

My Army Reserve Command asked me if I wanted to be the recruiter for Boston and I accepted. On January 2, 1973, I was placed on active duty with First Army, Fort Meade, and sent to recruiting school. Upon my return, I reported to the director of the Boston VA Center for duty. They set me up with a nice office in the JFK building and invited me to attend monthly staff meetings. I soon received support from George Medeiros, NSO of the AMVETS, and Stanly Hoy Jr. NSO of the DAV.

Within a few months, I was interviewing 30 to 40 veterans a month and meeting my 10% enlistment quota. I soon discovered that I was not the only Vietnam veteran who felt isolated. Many of the veterans came in to talk with me about their combat experiences after coming home from the war and the difficulties they had. In some cases, these veterans had no interest in actually joining the reserve; they just wanted to talk, and identified with my uniform and combat decorations.

I had one interview with a veteran that has always haunted me. He was dressed in a business suit and his face was scarred by severe burns. He told me that he had been a helicopter pilot and was shot down by NVA groundfire. His helicopter crashed and burned, and he spent over two years in Army hospitals undergoing skin grafts and recovering. He wanted to return to flying, but the Army had given him a medical discharge. Here was a man who had gone through a horrifying experience followed by years of intense pain who was willing to return to his comrades in combat.

I was beginning to identify with these warriors and I felt a strong bond with them. The more I talked to veterans, the more I realized that we all had two things in common. We missed the comradeship of military service and we all showed varying levels of what would later be identified as PTSD. These men told me things that they had not told anyone else since returning home. They felt comfortable talking with me. I soon became an experienced counselor and social worker, and helped put these men in touch with the professionals who could assist them. I was in daily contact with the VA counselors, the AMVETS, the DAV and the VFW, who all tried to reach out to the veterans.

I discovered that I was helping myself by helping these veterans. Working with them was a form of self-therapy. Sometime in the 1970s, my DAV contact, Stanly Hoy Jr., a marine combat veteran of the 1st Tank Battalion, suggested that I file a claim for PTSD. I knew that doing that could cause me to be disqualified from the military. I wanted to make a career out of the Army. I thanked him for his concern and opted not to file a claim for disability.

For the veterans who decided to enlist in the reserve, I found units close to their homes and got them started in their new units. Years later, some of them crossed my path and were well on their way to high-ranking positions, including direct commissions as officers and pilots.

After four years of duty on Project Search, I returned to my civilian job and part-time service in the Army Reserve. I began to get involved with veterans' organizations and veterans' affairs in my community, working with veterans and helping them file claims with the Veterans Administration. This helped me to establish social bonds and create lifelong friendships with some of them, which didn't just help us, but our families as well. Our wives supported each other, as they lived with our PTSD, and our children grew up together. We attended each other's family events over the years and have stuck together and supported each other. The bonds of comradeship that began in the jungles of Vietnam kept us together as brothers. For us, the Vietnam War never really ended.

In 1997 the VA granted me a 100% service-connected disability for Agent Orange exposure and PTSD. Prior to that, I held dual careers in the Army Reserve and the Federal Government, and graduated from the Boston State College evening degree program on the GI Bill. I retired from the Army Reserve as a master sergeant, infantry battalion staff NCO, and from the Defense Logistics Agency as a contract manufacturing specialist. I have attended many reunions with the 1st of the 9th Cavalry, meeting my old crewmates from Vietnam and keeping the memories of our old buddies alive in our hearts. At our 2015 9th Cav reunion, I took Peter Burbank with me. He got to meet some of his old Blues comrades and their families.

I am very proud to have served with the brave men of the 1st of the 9th Cavalry and I hope this story honors their service and sacrifice, and that future generations will know of their service to our great country, the United States of America.

Epilogue

Pete

I got my orders to ship home in November 1966. The war was almost over for me. I packed my duffle bag, gave away everything that I did not need, and got my summer short-sleeve uniform ready to ship out. Soon I was placed on a flight manifest and boarded the "Big Silver Bird" for the States. It was like a dream come true to be flying "out country" and leaving Vietnam behind.

I enjoyed my 30-day leave by going home to see my family, friends, and old World War II veteran Francis at the local VFW post. He was happy to see me again and told me how great I looked in my dress uniform with my airborne wings, combat infantry badge, and row of service ribbons. Francis was proud of me, and I was happy to have been able to follow in his footsteps as an airborne infantryman.

I decided to re-enlist and return for a second tour of Vietnam. On my second tour, I was an experienced combat soldier, so the Army used me to train new troops who were coming "in-country." That was okay by me as I did not miss life in the snake infested jungles on my first tour with the "Air Cav" in the Central Highlands. When my second tour ended, I returned to civilian life and tried to find a job, fit back into society, and get on with my life. That was the hardest experience I ever had. The economy was not offering well-paying jobs, and when I did manage to find one, I quickly got laid off and was back looking for a new job. I think I had about ten jobs during that time, and my prospects did not look good. I eventually found a decent job driving a delivery truck for a lumber company in Randolph, Massachusetts, on the south shore of Boston. One of my co-workers, Joe, had been an auxiliary police officer and he told me stories of how he would go out on patrols with the regular full-time police officers. I found this very interesting; it sounded like something I would like to do.

This may sound corny, but I thought I could do some good in society as a police officer helping people. "To protect and serve," as they say. Being a police officer was a lot like being a soldier. The job could be dangerous but rewarding. It would allow me to play a small part in making a difference in the lives of others. Not earth shattering, but a role I could play.

I was not able to get onto any police departments in Massachusetts. My older brother, who was in the U.S. Coast Guard up in Portland, Maine, suggested that I go up to his home and look into law enforcement jobs there. So, I left my parent's home in Hull, Massachusetts and went up country. I stayed with my brother until I was hired on January 2, 1972, by the Portland Police Department as a trainee patrolman. Because of my military knowledge of firearms, I was made range officer to train officers on how to improve their marksmanship.

It was a well-paying, steady job. I was able to keep my mind focused on police work and not on any bad memories of Vietnam. As time went on, the job got harder as I had to deal with stressful events while confronting the various "bad guys" and criminals in the city. On more than one occasion, I was forced to use my night stick or side arm to take a law breaker into custody. My confrontations with the enemy in Vietnam prepared me for the challenges of police work. It had its dangerous moments for sure, but the job kept me active and paid my bills.

I got married and began to raise a family, and I was eventually able to buy my own home out in Cumberland County not far from the city. In addition to my police work, I joined the Army Reserve as a part-time soldier. This was good for me as I met other veterans who, like myself, enjoyed the comradeship of being with fellow soldiers, especially when we went out in the field for our two-week annual training playing war games. The Army appreciated my Vietnam combat experience as I was able to train a new generation of young soldiers to the infantry trade. As a bonus to this job, I was around all the Army's latest weapons and got to use them in the field. As time went on, I managed to be promoted to the grade of sergeant first class (E-7) and the earnings helped me pay my mortgage. Plus, I was putting in my time in service to qualify for a military retirement at age 60.

Then in 1980, I began to have trouble sleeping, and when I did sleep, I had bad dreams of Vietnam. One dream I had was being out on patrol with my platoon and getting lost in the jungle, which happened to me in the Kim Son Valley battle of the Crow's Foot. I would wake up from these dreams in a cold sweat with my heart beating fast. This always disturbed and scared my wife; she thought I was going crazy. I began having flashbacks, especially if I heard a helicopter in the sky, like air ambulance aircraft or state police helicopters. If a big truck went by, I'd catch a whiff of the diesel exhaust smoke and that would remind me of the Army deuce and a half trucks and shit burning details in Vietnam. Even something as simple as rain pelting on the roof of my squad car at night on an overnight patrol, or on the roof at my home, would take me back to the Vietnam monsoons when it would rain for days and we would be soaking wet with no dry clothes, tiny rivers of rainwater running through our tents like streams. Even our cigarettes and matches got damp and we had to wrap them in plastic to keep them dry in our wet pockets. It was miserable being wet on a chilly night in the highland's mountains on an overnight ambush. Those old memories became more frequent as time went by. With the pressure of my job, raising a family, and the flashbacks, sometimes I would pop my cork and get angry, breaking dishes and yelling. I had no clue what was happening to me.

Eventually, I went to see my VA man to have a doctor check me out. That's when I found out I was suffering from post-traumatic stress disorder, or PTSD. For those who don't know, living with PTSD is like being on an emotional roller coaster. The VA started treating me for it and I had to keep that under my hat, as the police department would not want a cop who was suffering from PTSD. Many police officers would suffer a double case of PTSD if they were combat vets and had to deal with stress on the job. Even at home, it was pretty tough for them. That's how good marriages broke up, like mine. Living with a combat vet is not an easy thing for any woman. We vets can be difficult to deal with. Especially if we start self-medicating with booze. That's what happened to many World War II and Korean War combat vets after their wars. Many were hard drinkers and suffered from war stress. Just like my Francis from his World War II paratroop days. Back then, the VA had limited resources to deal with that problem. Today, we get pretty good care. I have no complaints about the VA care I get.

After I retired, the PTSD got worse as I had more time on my hands to think about my life experiences. I would sit around and feel sorry for myself, thinking how my marriage fell apart, and always blame myself for how it went down. I became more nervous and was disturbed by strange noises. My VA counselor told me I was suffering from a thing called "hyper-vigilant syndrome." Thinking back, I had many bouts of that but never knew what caused it.

Back in the 60s when I first came home, the VA had not yet started diagnosing PTSD. So, I just worked my way through it until they discovered it and began to treat it. It was that treatment that resulted in a program to help the recent war veterans coming back from the Afghanistan and Iraq wars.

A lot of folks back in the 70s saw us as crazy veterans. Movies and TV shows depicted us as a bunch of misfits and drug addicts who were all messed up. We got a bad rap. We were blamed for the way the war ended. Despite our sacrifices and valor, the public gave us no respect and employers were concerned about our mental stability on the job. Many of us were turned down for employment. Some draft dodger or college deferred kid got the job instead. That did not bode well for our self-esteem. Even some of my supervisors and co-workers wondered when I would eventually "crack up" on the job from my war experiences. It was a daily struggle to maintain control of my life and keep myself on track.

It was not until the movie actor Tom Selleck starred in "Magnum P.I.," a TV show about a Vietnam veteran, that Hollywood began to show us in a new light as good citizens. But by then the damage was done. The toll of all this had a major effect on us Vietnam veterans, but despite it, we worked hard and many of us overcame the negativity that came our way. Many Vietnam vets achieved much success and made us proud, like

General Colin Powell, Senator John McCain, and actor Dennis Franz as Detective Andy Sipowitz.

I am old now and I have accepted how my life has played out. I survived the war and got to live my life. There are 58,318 names on the Vietnam Wall in Washington, D.C., that represent kids like me who never got that chance. One of the best things from my time in Vietnam was that I got to know my long-time good friend Mike Kelley, who is the author of this book and encouraged me to contribute to this story of the 1st Squadron, 9th Cavalry in Vietnam. He even convinced me to attend a Vietnam reunion with him down in Columbus, Georgia, where I had taken my airborne training in 1965 at Fort Benning. I enjoyed seeing all my old Army buddies, and spending time with Mike and his family while staying at his home when we went to the 1/9th Reunion from Boston. I hope that our memories of Vietnam will provide some insight into what it was like for us to go off to war and return as changed human beings. As Civil War General Sherman once said, "War is Hell!"

List of Major Campaigns, 1965–1966

Operation *Clean House,* December 17–31, 1965. Mission: to support the 3rd Brigade, search and destroy, Suoi Ca Valley.

Operation *Matador,* January 1–17, 1966. Mission: to support the 1st and 2nd Brigades, search and destroy, Pleiku Province area.

Operation *Masher-White Wing,* January 25–March 6, 1966. Mission: to support the 1st, 2nd, and 3rd Brigades, search and destroy, Bong Son Area, Binh Dinh province.

Operation *Paul Revere,* May 9–June 20, 1966. Mission: to support the 2nd Brigade and Task Force 3rd Brigade, 25th Division out of LZ Oasis, Pleiku Province.

Operation *Hawthorne,* June 1966. Mission: to support 1st Cavalry operations around Dak To.

Operation *Hooker I,* June 1966. Mission: to support 2nd Brigade operations around Kontum.

Operation *Nathan Hale,* June 21–July 1, 1966. Mission: to support the 1st and 3rd Brigades, search and destroy operations around Tuy Hoa.

Operation *Paul Revere II,* August 1–25, 1966. Mission: to support the 2nd and 3rd Brigades and Task Force 3rd Brigade, 25th Division. Search and destroy out of LZ Oasis, Pleiku.

Operation *Byrd,* August 25, 1966–December 1, 1967. Mission: to support the 2nd Battalion, 7th Cavalry *Task Force Gary Owen* on security operations in the Phan Thiet area. Note: I only served on this operation for two months, August–September 1966, until my transfer back to base camp An Khe to be the crew chief of the OH-13S Scout helicopter, "The Green Hornet."

List of Weapons of War

U.S. Armed Forces

M-14 rifle, 7.62mm ammunition, 20 round magazine, used for basic training and sniper missions.

M-16E1 rifle, 5.56mm ammunition with M-7 Bayonet, 20 round magazine, used as an early helicopter door gun and infantry weapon. 1965–1966.

M-60 machine gun, 7.62mm, 100 round assault pack or long belts of ammo carried by gun crew and infantrymen for continuous fire. Also used as door gun on Huey Gunships. M-60C used as outboard guns on Huey Gunships. M-60D used as a pedestal mounted gun with dual hand grips on UH-1D Huey Infantry Slicks. This was the most reliable weapon in the U.S. Army inventory.

M-79 Grenade Launcher, 40mm ammunition, breech loaded. Could fire six rounds per minute and was very effective.

M-26 Fragmentation Grenade for close-in combat. M-18A1 Claymore Anti-Personnel Directional Mine.

Ithaca 37 Pump Action Shotgun, 12 to 20 gauge, 5 to 8 rounds in each magazine. Excellent jungle warfare weapon.

M 1911 semi-automatic .45 caliber pistol, 7 round box magazine. Excellent close combat weapon. Standard sidearm of helicopter door gunners and infantry patrol leaders.

Special .38 caliber revolver, 6 rounds in chamber for helicopter pilot crews. Easier to charge action and fire if wounded.

M2-60mm Light Infantry Mortar. Good for close-in fire support for an infantry platoon or squad. Known as the "Infantry's own Artillery."

M-29 81mm Heavy Mortar, used by the heavy weapons platoon of Delta Troop to provide indirect fire support for the Blues platoons of the 1/9th Cavalry.

M-40 106mm recoilless rifle mounted on a tripod or a M151 Mutt Jeep. Effective against enemy bunker complex and fortifications. Used by Delta Troop, 1/9th Cavalry in support of the Blues.

M-18 Smoke Grenades, used by helicopter crews and infantry to mark targets or to identify an LZ. Smoke colors were red, yellow, green, violet, and white.

North Vietnamese and Viet Cong Weapons

Chicom Type 56 SKS Semi-automatic Carbine, 7.62mm, 10 round magazine, rate of fire 30 rounds per minute.

Chicom Type AK-47 assault rifle, 7.62mm, 30 round magazine. On semi-auto fire, up to 40 rounds per minute. On full auto, up to 90 rounds per minute. This was a fearsome weapon that was very reliable, and deadly at almost any range. Highly respected.

Tokarev TT33 pistol and Chicom Type 51/54 7.62mm pistol (no safety lock) single action with 8 round box magazine. Standard side arm for NVA-VC Officers.

Soviet or Chicom Type 56 RPD light machine gun, 7.62mm caliber, air cooled, 100 round ammo drum belt fed. Deadly.

Soviet or Chicom Type 56 DPM light machine gun with bi-pod, 7.62mm, air cooled, top mounted drum magazine. Fearsome.

Soviet DSHK 1938 heavy machine gun, 12.7mm, Antiaircraft and ground support weapon. Mounted on two-wheel axle. Rate of fire 550 rounds per minute. Big pucker factor.

Infantry support weapons also used were mortars and anti-tank weapons made by the Soviets, Chicom, and captured USA and ARVN weapons.

Chicom Type 82 Medium Mortar. Mini Field Artillery.

Soviet M1937 and M1941 82mm Medium Mortar. Deadly weapon.

Chicom Type 62 57mm recoilless rifle. Effective against American military vehicles in an ambush and against strong points such as field bunkers.

Chicom Type 52 75mm recoilless rifle.

Soviet RPG-2 and Chicom B40 Anti-tank Weapon. Most common enemy weapon, very effective.

The two types of Viet Cong units used different weapons. The highly trained main force Viet Cong units were usually attached to an NVA command and used the same weapons as the NVA. The local force Viet Cong militia usually formed independent units which operated out of its home territory, much like National Guard units. Viet Cong local force militia weapons were a mixed bag of captured weapons and Soviet and Chicom weapons. Some were World War II American weapons that had been sold to the French Army under foreign military sales, and were used during the French Indo-China War from 1946 to 1954. A partial listing of these weapons includes French MAS 36 rifles, French MAT 49 submachine guns, and U.S. M2 Carbines. The VC also used U.S. M16 rifles, U.S. M-60 machine guns, U.S. 60 and 81mm mortars, hand grenade explosives, land mines, booby traps, and assorted handmade weapons. They could take a discarded Coke can and make a booby trap that could blow off your feet, legs, or arms. These weapons were very similar to the current slate of Iranian-style I.E.D.s made in Afghanistan and Iraq. They were very creative enemies. They also made their own ammunition in caves and hideouts. There was no doubt that bravery was not lacking in the NVA and VC Forces. They were hardcore warriors. Towards the end of the war, the NVA and VC were supplied with modern shoulder fired antiaircraft weapons that could shoot down helicopters and other types of aircraft.

1st Squadron, 9th Cavalry Commanders 1965–66

LTC. John B. Stockton—July–December 1965

LTC. Robert M. Shoemaker—December 1965–May 1966

LTC. James C. Smith—May–November 1966

LTC. A.T. Pumphry—November 1966–April 1967

Air Cavalry Units in Vietnam

Based on the success of the 1st Squadron, 9th Cavalry from 1965 to 1967, the U.S. Army established new Air Cavalry units and deployed them to Vietnam to support combat operations. Some were organic units assigned to the major divisions and commands, and some were independent units.

7th Squadron, 1st Cavalry—12th Aviation group in support of 9th Infantry Division

2nd Squadron, 17th Cavalry—101st Airborne Division (AIRMOBILE)

3rd Squadron, 17th Cavalry—II Field Force in support of 1st Infantry Division

7th Squadron, 17th Cavalry—17th Aviation Group in support of 4th Infantry Division

Independent Air Cavalry units were as follows

1st Squadron, 1st Cavalry; 2nd Squadron, 1st Cavalry; 1st Squadron, 4th Cavalry; 3rd Squadron, 4th Cavalry; 3rd Squadron, 9th Cavalry; 1st Squadron, 10th Cavalry; 11th Armored Cavalry.

A total of 14 independent Air Cavalry Troops were assigned to separate infantry brigades and commands.

A Closing Poem

Back in the late 1970s I used to like to visit the little book shops in Harvard Square in Cambridge, Massachusetts, to look for books about the Vietnam War in my attempt to understand and learn why I was there and what had happened. I found this small jewel of a book on poetry by author and Vietnam military police veteran Michael Casey, titled *Obscenities,* published by the Yale University Press. It was purchased along with my favorite Vietnam War book, *Street Without Joy,* by author Bernard Fall, published by Stackpole Books. I think all Vietnam veterans and students of the history of the Vietnam War should read both of these books to better understand the war and how it affected those of us who served in it.

A Bummer

We were going single file through his rice paddies, and the farmer started hitting the lead track with a rake. He wouldn't stop. The TC went to talk to him and the farmer tried to hit him too. So the tracks went sideways, side by side, through the guy's fields, instead of single file. Hard On, Proud Mary, Bummer, Wallace, Rosemary's Baby, The Ruttgers Road Runner, and Go Get Em – Done Got Em, went side by side, through the fields. If you have a farm in Vietnam, and a house in hell, sell the farm and go home.

Michael Casey
© Michael Casey

Photo Credits

Most of the photos in this book are by the author, Michael L. Kelley. Others are provided by the following individuals or organizations:
  Richard Denning—Scout Platoon
  Charles "Chuck" Knowlen—Blues Platoon Leader
  Joseph Waters—Gunship Pilot
  Frank Hiser—Gunship Pilot
  Jerry "Smoky" Schmotolocha—Blues Platoon RTO
  Hector Aviles—Delta Troop
  Bullwhip Squadron Website, 1st Squadron, 9th Cavalry
  charlietroopcav.org, Webmaster Grover Wright
  William Joseph Nave
  Textron-Bell Helicopters Media Office—David Woolfe
  Cover Artwork Image—"Guns Up" by Joe Kline Aviation Art
  First Cavalry Division Association Gift Shop

Selected Bibliography

Brennan, Matthew. *Headhunters*. Presidio Press, Pocket Books, 1988.

Brennan, Matthew. *Brennan's War: Vietnam 1965–1969*. Presidio Press, Pocket Books, 1989.

Brennan, Matthew. *Hunter-Killer Squadron: Aero-Weapons, Aero-Scouts, Aero-Rifles, Vietnam 1965–1972*. Presidio Press, Pocket Books, 1992.

Casey, Michael. *Obscenities*. Yale University Press, 1972.

Coleman, J.D. *Pleiku: The Dawn of Helicopter Warfare in Vietnam*. St. Martins Press, 1988.

Fall, Bernard B. *Street Without Joy: Indochina at War, 1946–54*. Stackpole Books, 1961.

Nave, William Joseph. *Tears of a Soldier's Son: One Son's Journey to Healing*. 2015.

Ninh, Bao. *The Sorrow of War*. Riverhead Books, New York, 1996.

Roberts, E. G., MG., *The 1st Air Cavalry Division: Vietnam, August 1965 to December 1969*. Dia Nippon Printing Co., Tokyo, Japan.

Tolson, John J., Lieutenant General. *Vietnam Studies: Airmobility 1961–1971*. Department of the Army, Washington, D.C., 1973.

Glossary of Terms

AIT	Advanced individual training.
AMVETS	American veterans.
AO	Area of operations.
APC	Armored personnel carrier.
ARA	Air rocket artillery.
ARVN	Army of South Vietnam.
AWOL	Absent without leave.
BCT (unit)	Basic combat training unit.
CIB	Combat Infantry Badge.
CP	Command post.
C-rations	Pre-canned foods.
CS	Riot gas chemicals.
CWO	Chief warrant officer.
DAV	Disabled American veterans.
DEROS	Date expected return overseas.
DZ	Drop zone.
EM	Enlisted men.
FAC pilot	Forward air control pilot.
GP (Tent)	General-purpose tent.
GT	General test.
Hop	Free ride on military aircraft.
IFR conditions	Instrument flight rules.
KIA	Killed in action.
KP	Kitchen police (duty).
Latrine	Bathroom.
LZ	Landing zone.
MACV	Military Assistance Command, Vietnam.

MOS	Military Occupation Specialty.
NCO	Non-commissioned officer.
NFG	New friggin' guy.
NOE	Nap of the earth.
NSO	National service officer.
NVA	North Vietnamese Army.
OCS	Officers' training school.
OJT	On the job training.
PFC	Private first class.
PLF	Parachute landing fall.
POV	Privately owned vehicle.
PRC-10 Radio	Prick-10 Radio.
PSP	Perforated steel planking (Marston Mat).
PT	Physical training.
PX	post exchange.
Repo-Depot	Replacement depot.
ROK	Republic of Korea.
RTO	Radio Telephone Operator.
SITREP	Situation report.
SP Pack	Sundry Pack provided to soldiers which contained assorted supplies such as cartons of cigarettes, cigars, candy bars, gum, pens, stationery, etc.
TAC AIR	Tactical air support.
TAC	Tactical training leader of warrant officer cadets.
TDY	Temporary duty away from unit.
TOC	Tactical communications center.
VA counselor	Veterans Administration representative for veterans' assistance.
VFR flying weather	Instrument flight rules for visual conditions.
VFW Club	Veterans of Foreign Wars Club.
WIA	Wounded in action.
Willie Peter	White phosphorus.
WO	Warrant officer.
WP grenades	Willie Peter (white phosphorus) grenades.